Chá[illegible] de ([illegible]s

Claude Catherine Terrier
Curator of Antiquités and Objets d'Art, Director of Château de Carrouges

Olivier Renaudeau
Heritage curator with the regional service of the Inventaire général de Basse-Normandie

"The interior of the château is at least as expressive as the façades. [...] Here resides great simplicity of olden times, conspiring with bombastic magnificence. The hallways are covered in lime, whilst the ceremonial chambers are highly embellished ..." (Jean de La Varende, *En parcourant la Normandie*, 1953).

Bordering Normandy and Maine, nestled in between the forests of Andaine and Écouves, the château de Carrouges is living proof of the care proffered by three generations of high-ranking dignitaries to a vast estate originally built for defence and transformed into a place of pleasure.

During more than five centuries, they were able to maintain their seigniory and enrich their residence, one of the most extensive in Normandy. The austerity of this edifice (constructed from the late 14th to late-16th century) is tempered by the warmth of its red-and-black bricks and by the charm of its park. Its architecture, interior décors and furniture evoke the daily life of the French aristocracy who, despite wars and revolutions, tirelessly pursued their comings-and-goings between city and country, between official responsibilities and improvements to the land.

Notre-Dame de Chartres, construite aux XIIe et XIIIe siècles, présente un décor sculpté et des vitraux exceptionnels ainsi qu'un trésor. Du haut de la tour dite « Jehan de Beauce », on peut admirer un panorama unique sur la ville et la Beauce.

horaires sous réserve

Ouvert tous les jours sauf dimanche matin
1er mars au 30 avril
9h30 à 11h30 et 14h à 17h
2 mai au 31 août
9h à 18h
le dimanche 13h à 18h30
1er septembre au 31 octobre
9h30 à 11h30 et 14h à 17h
1er novembre au 28/29 février
10h à 11h30 et 14h à 16h.

Fermé
les 1er janvier, 1er mai, le lundi de Pentecôte après-midi, le 25 décembre.

Accès
depuis Le Mans A11, sortie 3, N10 ; depuis Paris A11, sortie 2, N10 ; de Rouen ou Orléans N154. Train direct de Paris-Montparnasse.

Accueil
visite libre de la tour (300 marches, 60 m) et de la cathédrale. Réservation demandée pour les groupes.

Notre Dame de Chartres, constructed in the 12th and 13th c., has carved decoration and some outstanding century stained glass windows and treasure-house. From the top of the tower called "Jehan de Beauce" there is a unique panoramic view of the town and the Beauce.

times may vary

Open daily except Sunday morning
1 March to 30 April
9.30 to 11.30 am
and 2 to 5 pm
2 May to 31 August
9 am to 6 pm
Sunday 1 to 6.30 pm
1 September to 31 October
9.30 to 11.30 am
and 2 to 5 pm
1 November to 28/29 February
10 to 11.30 am
and 2 to 4 pm.

Closed
1 January, 1 May, Whit Monday afternoon, 25 December.

Access
from Le Mans, A11, exit 3, N10; from Rouen or Orleans N154; Direct train from Paris-Montparnasse.

Facilities
Unaccompanied visit to the tower (300 steps, 60 m) and cathedral. Groups by prior reservation only.

Notre-Dame de Chartres, errichtet im 12./13. Jh., besitzt weltberühmte Fensterwände und skulpturale Dekorationen, sowie einen Kirchenschatz. Von dem Turm "Jehan de Beauce" bietet sich ein einzigartiges Panorama auf die Stadt und das Beauce-Gebiet.

Änderungen vorbehalten

Geöffnet täglich außer sonntags morgens
1. März-30. April
9h30-11h30 und 14h-17h
2. Mai-31. August
9h-18h
sonntags 13h-18h30
1. September-31. Oktober
9h30-11h30 und 14h-17h
1. November-28./29. Februar
10h-11h30 und 14h-16h.

Geschlossen
1. Januar, 1. Mai, Pfingstmontag nachmittags, 25. Dezember.

Anreise
Von Le Mans A11, Abfahrt 3, N10; von Paris A11, Abfahrt 2, N10; von Rouen oder Orléans N154. Direkter Zug von Paris-Montparnasse.

Angebot
Freie Besichtigung des Turms (300 Stufen, 60 m) und der Kathedrale. Für Gruppen Voranmeldung erbeten.

photo F. G. Osorio, Ville de Chartres **impression** dugas-martin, mars 2002 **conception** LM communiquer

Centre des monuments nationaux
Cathédrale de Chartres
28000 Chartres
tél. 02 37 21 22 07
fax 02 37 36 08 80

www.monum.fr

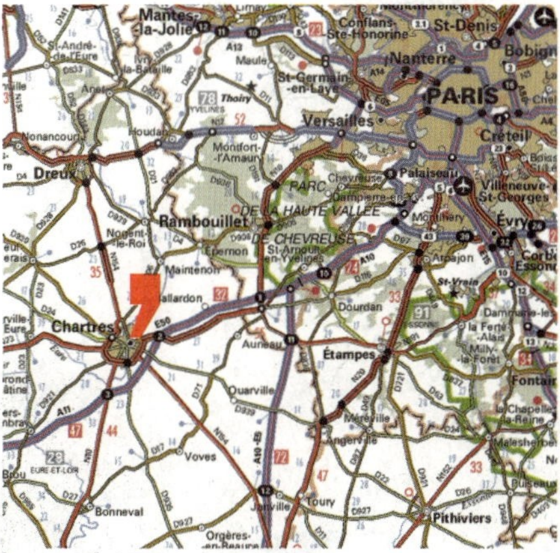

tours de la cathédrale de Chartres

EURE-ET-LOIR • CENTRE

monum,

château d'Azay-le-Rideau

VAL-DE-LOIRE • TOURAINE

Bâti sur une île au milieu de l'Indre, Azay-le-Rideau fut édifié sous François Ier par un de ses financiers, Gilles Berthelot. Émergeant au centre d'un parc romantique, le château conserve une remarquable unité de style : une alliance parfaite d'éléments traditionnels et d'italianisme. Le décor des salles entièrement meublées, retrace la vie des plus illustres hôtes des lieux à travers les siècles.

horaires sous réserve

Ouvert tous les jours
1er avril au 30 juin et
1er septembre au 31 octobre
9h30 à 18h
1er juillet au 31 août
9h30 à 19h
1er novembre au 31 mars
10h à 12h30 et 14h à 17h30, dernier accès 45 mn avant.

Fermé
les 1er janvier, 1er mai, 25 décembre.

Accès
depuis Paris A10 Paris-Bordeaux, sortie 14 Joué-les-Tours.

Services
visite libre, audioguidée ou commentée. Parcours-spectacle nocturne, tous les soirs de mai à septembre : "Les Imaginaires d'Azay-le-Rideau".

Built on an island in the middle of the Indre, Azay-le-Rideau was constructed in the reign of François I by one of his financiers, Gilles Berthelot. Rising up in the centre of a romantic park, the château retains an extraordinary unity of style: a perfect combination of traditional elements and Italicism. The décor of the fully-furnished rooms, recounts the life of the most illustrious occupants of the house over the centuries.

times may vary

Open every day
1 April to 30 June and
1 September to 31 October
9.30 am to 6 pm
1 July to 31 August
9.30 am to 7 pm
1 November to 31 March
10 am to 12.30 pm and 2 to 5.30 pm, last admission 45 mins before.

Closed
1 January, 1 May, 25 December.

Access
from Paris A10 Paris-Bordeaux, exit 14 Joué-les-Tours.

Facilities
unaccompanied visits, with optional audioguide or guided tour. Night-time promenade show, every evening from May to September: "Les Imaginaires d'Azay-le-Rideau".

Das Schloss wurde unter Franz I. von dessen Schatzmeister Gilles Berthelot auf einer Insel im Fluss Indre in einem romantischen Park erbaut. Es ist in einer bemerkenswerten stilistischen Einheitlichkeit erhalten: die Verbindung traditioneller und italianisierender Elemente ist perfekt. Anhand des Dekors der vollständig möblierten Säle wird das Leben der berühmtesten Gäste im Laufe der Jahrhunderte nacherzählt.

Änderungen vorbehalten

Geöffnet täglich
1. April - 30. Juni und
1. September - 31 Oktober
9h30 - 18h
1. Juli - 31. August
9h30 - 19h
1 November - 31. März
10 - 12.30 und 14h - 17h30, letzter Einlaß 45 Min. vor Ende.

Geschlossen
am 1. Januar, 1. Mai, 25. Dezember.

Anreise
von Paris A10 Paris-Bordeaux, Abfahrt 14 Joué-les-Tours.

Angebot
Freie Besichtigung, Kopfhörerführung und Führung. Nächtlicher Erlebnisrundgang jeden Abend vom Mai bis September: "Les Imaginaires d'Azay-le-Rideau".

Centre des monuments nationaux
Château d'Azay-le-Rideau
37190 Azay-le-Rideau
tél 02 47 45 42 04
fax 02 47 45 26 61

www.monum.fr

photo Ph. Berthé © Centre des monuments nationaux, Paris **impression** dugas-martin, février 2001 **conception** LM communiquer

Bâti sur une île au milieu de l'Indre, Azay-le-Rideau fut édifié sous François Ier par un de ses financiers, Gilles Berthelot. Émergeant au centre d'un parc romantique, le château conserve une remarquable unité de style : une alliance parfaite d'éléments traditionnels et d'italianisme. Le décor des salles entièrement meublées, retrace la vie des plus illustres hôtes des lieux à travers les siècles.

horaires sous réserve

Ouvert tous les jours
1er avril au 30 juin et
1er septembre au 31 octobre
9h30 à 18h
1er juillet au 31 août
9h30 à 19h
1er novembre au 31 mars
10h à 12h30 et 14h à 17h30, dernier accès 45 mn avant.

Fermé
les 1er janvier, 1er mai, 25 décembre.

Accès
depuis Paris A10 Paris-Bordeaux, sortie 14 Joué-les-Tours.

Services
visite libre, audioguidée ou commentée. Parcours-spectacle nocturne, tous les soirs de mai à septembre : "Les Imaginaires d'Azay-le-Rideau".

Built on an island in the middle of the Indre, Azay-le-Rideau was constructed in the reign of François I by one of his financiers, Gilles Berthelot. Rising up in the centre of a romantic park, the château retains an extraordinary unity of style: a perfect combination of traditional elements and Italicism. The décor of the fully-furnished rooms, recounts the life of the most illustrious occupants of the house over the centuries.

times may vary

Open every day
1 April to 30 June and
1 September to 31 October
9.30 am to 6 pm
1 July to 31 August
9.30 am to 7 pm
1 November to 31 March
10 am to 12.30 pm and 2 to 5.30 pm, last admission 45 mins before.

Closed
1 January, 1 May, 25 December.

Access
from Paris A10 Paris-Bordeaux, exit 14 Joué-les-Tours.

Facilities
unaccompanied visits, with optional audioguide or guided tour. Night-time promenade show, every evening from May to September: "Les Imaginaires d'Azay-le-Rideau".

Das Schloss wurde unter Franz I. von dessen Schatzmeister Gilles Berthelot auf einer Insel im Fluss Indre in einem romantischen Park erbaut. Es ist in einer bemerkenswerten stilistischen Einheitlichkeit erhalten: die Verbindung traditioneller und italianisierender Elemente ist perfekt. Anhand des Dekors der vollständig möblierten Säle wird das Leben der berühmtesten Gäste im Laufe der Jahrhunderte nacherzählt.

Änderungen vorbehalten

Geöffnet täglich
1. April - 30. Juni und
1. September - 31 Oktober
9h30 - 18h
1. Juli - 31. August
9h30 - 19h
1 November - 31. März
10 - 12.30 und 14h - 17h30, letzter Einlaß 45 Min. vor Ende.

Geschlossen
am 1. Januar, 1. Mai, 25. Dezember.

Anreise
von Paris A10 Paris-Bordeaux, Abfahrt 14 Joué-les-Tours.

Angebot
Freie Besichtigung, Kopfhörerführung und Führung. Nächtlicher Erlebnisrundgang jeden Abend vom Mai bis September: "Les Imaginaires d'Azay-le-Rideau".

Centre des monuments nationaux
Château d'Azay-le-Rideau
37190 Azay-le-Rideau
tél 02 47 45 42 04
fax 02 47 45 26 61

www.monum.fr

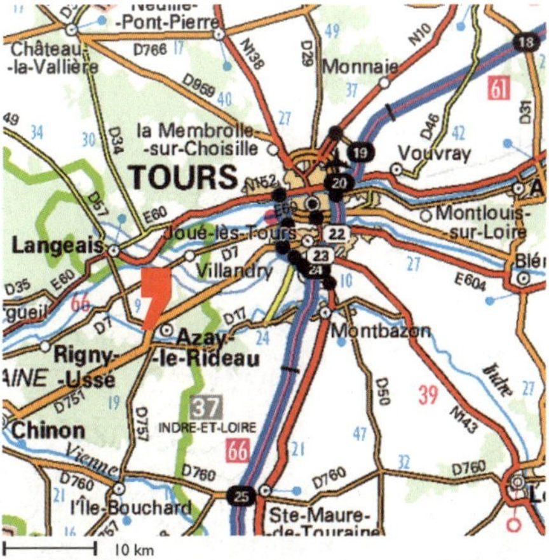

photo Ph. Berthé © Centre des monuments nationaux, Paris impression dugas-martin, février 2001 conception LM communiquer

monum,

château d'Azay-le-Rideau

VAL-DE-LOIRE • TOURAINE

L'abbaye Notre-Dame-du-Bec connut un grand rayonnement intellectuel au XIe siècle. Reconstruit aux XVIIe et XVIIIe siècles par la congrégation de Saint-Maur, le monastère est dominé par la haute tour Saint-Nicolas, vestige du XVe siècle. Une communauté de moines bénédictins y est installée depuis 1948.

Ouvert tous les jours
1er juin au 30 septembre
10h30 à 21h
(visites à 10h30, 15h, 21h)
1er octobre au 31 mai
10h30 à 21h
(visites à 10h30, 21h).

Accès
de Paris ou Rouen, A13 sortie 24, N 138 direction Bernay, puis D39. De Caen, N13 direction Evreux, D130, puis D39.

Accueil
visite libre et commentée (sauf les mardis et le 25 décembre).

Notre-Dame-du-Bec Abbey enjoyed a period of great intellectual influence in the 11th century. Rebuilt in the 17th and 18th centuries by the order of Saint-Maur, the monastery is dominated by the tall Saint-Nicolas tower, a vestige from the 15th century. A community of Benedictine monks has been in residence here since 1948.

Open every day
1 June to 30 September
10.30 am - 9 pm
(tours at 10.30 am, 3 pm, 9 pm)
1 October to 31 May
10.30 am - 9 pm
(tours at 10.30 am, 9 pm).

Access
from Paris or Rouen, A13 exit 24, N 138 towards Bernay, then D39. From Caen, N13 towards Evreux, D 130, then D39.

Facilities
unaccompanied and guided tour (except for Tuesdays and 25 December).

Die Abtei Notre-Dame-du-Bec hatte im 11. Jh. bedeutenden Einfluss auf das geistige Leben. Das Kloster wurde im 17. und 18. Jh. von der Kongregation St. Maur wieder aufgebaut. Überragt wird es vom hohen Turm Saint-Nicolas, der aus dem 15. Jh. stammt. Seit 1948 lebt hier eine Gemeinschaft von Benediktinermönchen.

Geöffnet täglich
1. Juni bis 30. September
10h30 bis 21h
(Führungen um 10h30, 15h, 21h)
1. Oktober bis 31. Mai
10h30 bis 21h
(Führungen um 10h30, 21h).

Anreise
von Paris oder Rouen A13 Ausfahrt 24, N138 Richtung Bernay, dann D39. Von Caen N13 Richtung Evreux, D130, dann D39.

Angebot
Freie Besichtigung und Führung (außer Dienstags und 25. Dezember).

photo B. Acloque © Centre des monuments nationaux, Paris **impression** Imprimerie de l'Indre, décembre 2000 **conception** LM communiquer

Centre des monuments nationaux
Abbaye Notre-Dame-du-Bec
27800 Le Bec-Hellouin
tél. 02 32 43 72 60
fax 02 32 44 96 69

www.monuments.fr

carte n° 901 © IGN 1999, autorisation n° 90-0014

monum,

monum,

abbaye du Bec-Hellouin

EURE • FRANCE

Carrouges, Blosset, Le Veneur
Three families and one château

Owners of Carrouges

Marriages

Jeanne de Carrouges
(? -1421)

Jeanne de Cagny

1438

Robert de Cagny
(1386-1424)

Guillaume Blosset
(1386-1424)

Michelle Gabrielle du Gué de Bagnols
(? -1756)

Anne Favier du Boulay (? -1704)

Catherine de Bassompierre

1699

1663

1608

Jacques Tanneguy III Le Veneur
(1671-1748)

François Le Veneur
(1641-1687)

1638

Henry Le Veneur
(? -1687)

Claude Rouault
(? -1669)

Michelle Julie Bouchard d'Esparbès de Lussan (1715-1742)

Charlotte Henriette de Verdelin
(? -1834)

Félicité de Jupilles
(? -1834)

1730

1778

1801

Jacques Tanneguy IV Le Veneur
(1700-1777)

Alexis Paul Michel Le Veneur (General Le Veneur)
(1746-1833)

Alexis Tanneguy VI Le Veneur
(1779-1851)

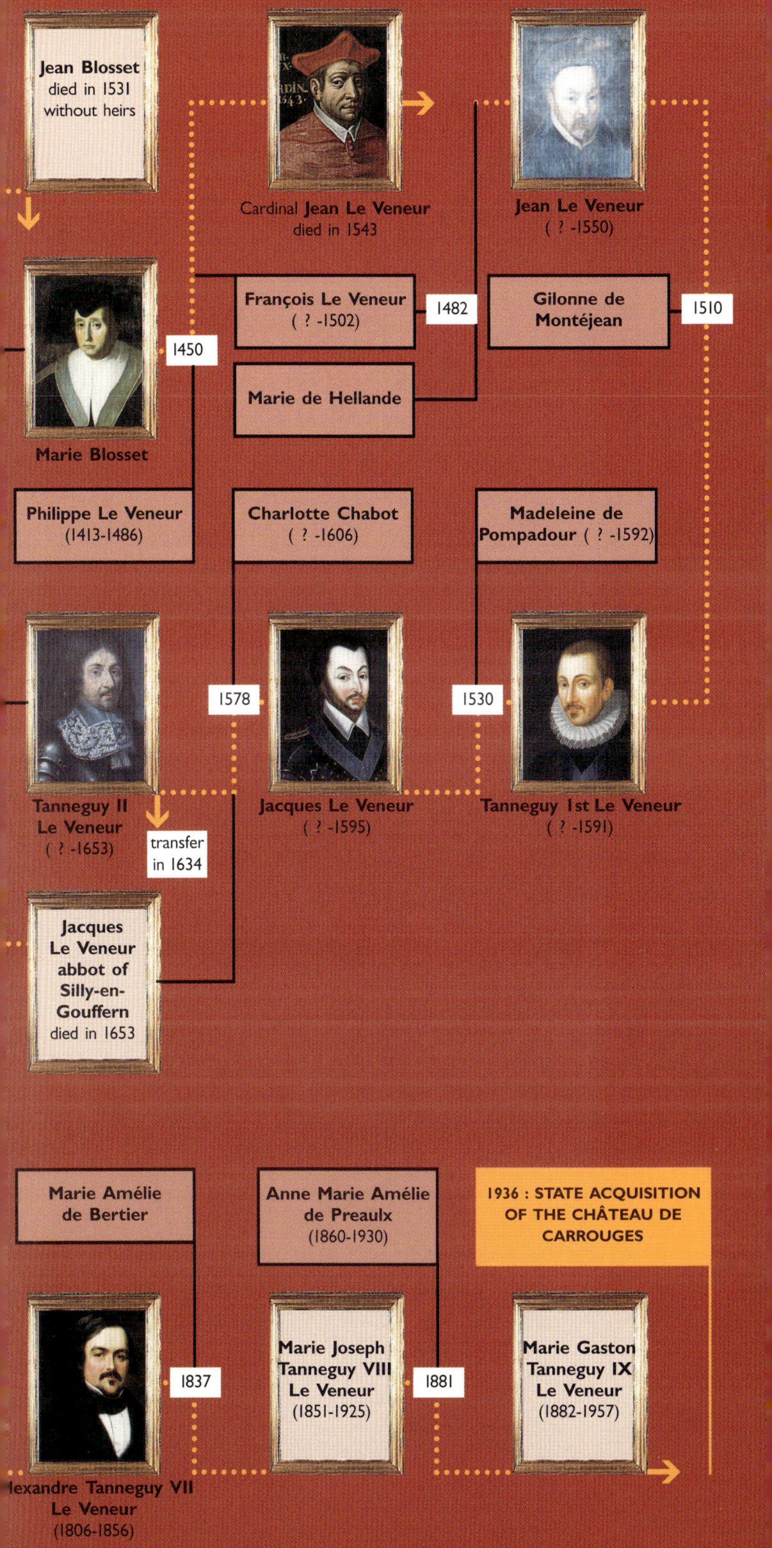
Jean Blosset died in 1531 without heirs
Cardinal Jean Le Veneur died in 1543
Jean Le Veneur (? -1550)
François Le Veneur (? -1502)
1482
Gilonne de Montéjean
1510
1450
Marie de Hellande
Marie Blosset
Philippe Le Veneur (1413-1486)
Charlotte Chabot (? -1606)
Madeleine de Pompadour (? -1592)
1578
1530
Tanneguy II Le Veneur (? -1653)
Jacques Le Veneur (? -1595)
Tanneguy 1st Le Veneur (? -1591)
transfer in 1634
Jacques Le Veneur abbot of Silly-en-Gouffern died in 1653
Marie Amélie de Bertier
Anne Marie Amélie de Preaulx (1860-1930)
1936 : STATE ACQUISITION OF THE CHÂTEAU DE CARROUGES
1837
Marie Joseph Tanneguy VIII Le Veneur (1851-1925)
1881
Marie Gaston Tanneguy IX Le Veneur (1882-1957)
lexandre Tanneguy VII Le Veneur (1806-1856)

The first lords

(1150-1438)

Arms of the lords of Carrouges, the most ancient of which are described in the 14th century within the armorial of Martin Carbonnel, king of Charles le Mauvais's heralds: "My sire Jehan de Carouiges, red with silver – or gold – fleur(s) de lis".

Carrouges derives from the name given by the Romans to a site established at the crossroads of two ancient byways. The first historic mention associated with this name, in 1136, records a three-day siege maintained by Geoffroi Plantagenêt, comte d'Anjou, who wanted to conquer the province. Carrouges was one of multiple border stations on the southern frontier of the Norman duchy. This military keep at the edge of the forests (Écouves and Andaines in Normandy, Multonne and Monaye in Maine) had been established in a defensive marshy site.

The first lords of Carrouges, cited in charters♦ as early as 1150, do not appear to have left a trace on the site until the epoch of Jean IV who might have built the donjon. In 1383, he fought in Flanders at the side of the comte d'Alençon against the English.

The donjon, marked out by its machicolations, bears witness to the fortified château of Carrouges.

♦ ***Charter:*** *licensor act for franchises and privileges, document recording transactions. The ensemble of charters constitute the charter room.*

Then he accompanied Jean de Vienne, captain at Honfleur, in an expedition to the English and Scottish coasts. The honour of his wife having been gravely compromised whilst he was in the king's service in Paris, Jean IV succeeded in bringing the affair before the Parlement (High Court of Justice) of Paris who ordered a judicial duel in 1386, to be the last of its kind in France (see p. 9).

"Plantagenêt enamel". This funerary effigy depicts the living Geoffroi Plantagenêt, comte d'Anjou, father of Henri II, duc de Normandie and King of England. He carries a triangular shield emblazoned with azur and gold rampant lions: this is the most ancient figuration of an hereditary blazon. 64,2 x 34,1 cm. Second half of the 12th century (Le Mans, Musée de Tessé).

The oldest feature in the dwelling is the donjon which occupies the approximate centre of the north-west wing of the château, to the left of the present entry. If its brick fabric and bay treatment (subsequently enlarged) hardly distinguish it from the rest of the building, the crowning of the machicolations♦ in running brick arcs resting on granite corbels♦ (continuing, too, along the interior of the buildings which were added later) testify to a preoccupation with defence, more evident than in other parts of the château.

This square "central-block tower" is reinforced at the west corner by a block of the same shape, but smaller, whilst the south turret, since disappeared, housed a spiral staircase permitting access to the upper floors. It was composed of three storeys, not counting the attic, perhaps once habitable.

On the ground floor, the entrance opens onto the communal room which doubled as a kitchen. A corridor allows access to the west shooting chamber. The position of the loopholes fitted out on this storey indicates that this donjon was isolated, or that it certainly occupied a corner of the original residence which might have had a regular quadrilateral corresponding to half the present château. The first storey (closed to visitors) undoubtedly comprised a hall or single room, linked to a *garde-robe* [dressing-room] installed in the west tower equipped with latrines. More intimate and easier to heat apartments were installed there at the beginning of the 19th century. On the renovated second storey, one recognizes the original disposition of rooms, analogous to those on the first storey.

Although well conceived, this cramped abode certainly did not itself constitute the Château de Carrouges in the 14th century. Other lodgings undoubtedly leaned up against the exterior defence walls to the north- and south-east of the building,

♦ ***Machicolations:*** *overhanging openings from which to throw projectiles.*

♦ ***Corbel:*** *projecting stone on a wall acting as a support.*

but only a few fragments survive in the lower sections of the later constructions.

After the English captured Honfleur in 1419, the land of Carrouges was confiscated by king Henry V. Submitting to the English sovereign, Robert de Carrouges resumed possession of his property. Later, to live down this treason, he raised a troop and travelled the length and breadth of Normandy in the service of the future Charles VII. He appeared on the list of the one hundred and nineteen valiant defenders of the Mont-Saint-Michel. Henry VI of England consequently confiscated his land in the bailiwicks of Cotentin and Rouen. Robert was slain at Verneuil, fighting alongside count Jean d'Alençon who was taken prisoner. The king of England rewarded his partisans by distributing his vanquished enemies' properties, the land of Carrouges falling to Jean de Montoire who appears to have returned it shortly thereafter.

The Carrouges dynasty ended with Jeanne, daughter of Robert, who married Robert de Cagny.

The existing village of Carrouges dominates the château, perhaps occupying the site of the *oppidum* which Orderic Vital testifies to in his mention of the 1136 siege.

The "tithe stone"

This imposing granite block, hollowed out with four cavities, is in fact a standard reference for diverse measures in use during transactions. As owners of markets and fairgrounds, the lords of Carrouges controlled commerce. After the Hundred Years War, the Blossets had to prove to the royal authority that they were indeed responsible for the four annual fairs and weekly market. Louis XI's decree (which reconfirmed their rights) also set Wednesday (replacing Sunday) as market day, since then not altered. The stone no doubt dates from this period. It indicates the "Carrouges measure" for liquids, grains, flour or salt. Measures varied from one seigniory to another. Colbert had wished, unsuccessfully, to put this confusion into order: "One king, one law, one weight, one measure". With the metric system established by the Convention, such idiosyncrasies came to an end.

Equestrian combat of the 15th century, miniature extracted from the *Chronique de Bertrand Du Guesclin, roman d'Ogier le Danois* (Chantilly, Musée Condé).

The duel of Carrouges (1386)

This judicial duel was the last of its kind ordered by the Parlement (High Court of Justice) of Paris. Such ultimate recourse to decide the truthfulness of an accusation had become an exception after the 13th century. In his absence during the winter of 1385, the lord of Carrouges confined his very young wife to his mother's care. Upon his return, she alleged that equerry Jacques Le Grix, her husband's friend and duc d'Alençon's favourite, forced her against her will. The sire of Carrouges demanded reparation to his honour before his suzerain at Alençon. His request was refused. In favour with Charles VI, Carrouges then succeeded in having his case submitted on final appeal to the Parlement of Paris. A duel was ordered, set for Saturday, 29 December 1386 in Paris, presided over by the young king.

According to very ancient ritual, the confessed protagonists attended mass, took communion and swore before God and king to combat loyally. First on the saddle, then dismounted, Carrouges was wounded. Le Grix fell. Carrouges placed his foot on his chest and demanded of the king if he could deliver justice. "*Faites justice*". The sword pierced the body of Le Grix; he was led to the gallows. It was rumoured that Le Grix was not guilty. An adventurer, on his death bed, seems to have confessed responsibility for the infamy. At the conclusion of the combat, the sire of Carrouges departed for the Holy Land, the lady of Carrouges retreating to a convent. The tale is to be found in all chronicles of the period: the *Annales de France*, the *Chroniques* of Froissart, the *Chroniques de Saint-Denis*. In his *Discours sur les duels* two centuries later, Brantôme describes the combat depicted by a tapestry in Charles IX's Blois apartments. In the 18th century, a jurist allied to the Veneur family, chancellor Hénault, Parlement president, recalled this affair in his *Abrégé chronologique de l'histoire de France*. Doubtless it was this text which inspired Alexander Dumas' *La Dame de Carrouges*, its manuscript now lost.

The Blossets

(1438-1531)

The Blossets feature in the armorial of Jehan de Courtois, herald in the service of Louis d'Anjou, king of Jerusalem (15th century). "The Bloces [sic], pale azur and gold, with red chevrons charged with watered silver fasces".

Jeanne de Cagny, heiress of Carrouges, transferred this seigniory to the Blosset family upon her 1438 marriage to Guillaume, called *Le Borgne or The One-Eyed*. Lord of Saint-Pierre-en-Caux, he was first chamberlain to Jean II, duc d'Alençon, then cupbearer to king Charles VI and chamberlain to Charles VII. Allied to the kings of France, he proved himself skilful and efficient during the wars against England.
Upon his death, the estate returned to Jean, his eldest son, grand seneschal of Normandy, bailiff of Rouen, councillor and chamberlain to Louis XI. He was responsible for the construction of the main residential block carrying his name which notably improved the comfort of his residence. There he received the king in 1473. It was he, with his wife Marguerite de Derval, who founded the canonical community of Carrouges in 1480. The Blosset wing is a rectangular main block completed, at the north and east angles, by two narrow oblique pavilions.

The Blosset wing appears on the left, framed by its two pavilions on the bias. Émile Sagot lithograph, circa 1850.

The novelty of this construction did not contravene the original plan of the château: the main section of this wing is, in fact, built upon the old curtain-walls between two bastions, as confirmed by the somewhat irregular granite masonry which served as its foundations. The oblique pavilions are themselves entirely constructed of brick, but are contemporary with this new central block.

Detail of the 1711 plan, conserved at the château. Here one sees the tower in the middle of the chapel destroyed in the late 18th century.

Abutting one corner of the courtyard, a rather monumental, hexagonal stair tower, called "the tower of the charter room", serves the upper floors. It is coifed by a lofty room accessible from a small turret wedged against it. It was there that the château archives were conserved until the State acquisition in 1936. Opposite the moats, a second exterior construction, square in plan, was occupied by a chapel on the first storey. It was destroyed by General Le Veneur, likely in 1793. Originally, the entry into the residential corps was through the door situated to the right of the stair tower which gave access to the guards room. From

this room, one could either head toward the present kitchen to the right, or take the spiral staircase inside the tower to the left, to reach the three upstairs rooms. The first floor of this new residence was composed of two full symmetrical apartments. The central room (presently the north salon) which one arrived at from the spiral staircase was once the upstairs public room, used as a vestibule to the chapel, an antechamber or reception room. On each side stretched two "*chambres de parement*♦" (Louis XI's chamber and ceremonial antechamber), more intimate rooms where certain distinguished guests could be received. The rooms were extended, in each of the oblique pavilions, by a "*chambre de retrait*♦", linked to the *garde-robe* equipped with latrines. Such spatial hierarchy, from public to private, is characteristic of grand Medieval aristocratic dwellings. This disposition was modified by the arrangement of a continuous corridor and by the transformation of the central room (north salon) into a chamber which a partition wall divided so as to furnish an indispensable *garde-robe*.

During his lifetime, being without heir, Jean Blosset ceded his estate and château, thus enlarged, to his sister Marie. He died in 1531.

♦ ***Chambre de parement:*** *(literally 'ornamented room') a room of substantial proportions, situated upstairs, where the lord received close friends or distinguished guests.*

♦ ***Chambre de retrait:*** *(literally 'withdrawal chamber') a small intimate room, for the owner's use, often situated in a tower or annex pavilion.*

The donjon and the spiral staircase of the Blosset wing recall the Medieval origins of the Château de Carrouges.

Left
View of the back of the chasuble.

Centre
Detail of one of the *écus* with the arms of the Carrouges sewn onto the back of the chasuble.

Right
Detail of the embroidered decoration: a large gothic "E", monogram of Edward IV, is framed with the crowns of France (fleurs-de-lys) and of England.

The Carrouges chasuble

The Musée départemental d'Art sacré of Orne holds a liturgical vestment presently known as the "*chasuble de Carrouges*" whose provenance is traced to the former collegiate church of the château. Originally cut in a bell-shape, this ornament hung down lower under the arms and was most likely fashioned into its present shape in the 17th century.

The orphrey♦, which forms a large cross across the back of the chasuble, displays exceptional embroidered ornamentation: two bands of blue-and-burgundy velvet containing the devise of the English monarchy, "God and My Right", hem in white roses alternating with the crowns of England and France framing a large "E".

These emblematic motifs allow one to associate this work with the English king Edward IV (1442-1483), one of the protagonists in the War of the Roses. The green-silk damask support, with its characteristic stems of embroidered thistles, is also English fabric of the second half of the 15th century.

One might ask by what fate the lords of Carrouges came into possession of this royal chasuble. The date of its arrival at the château is unknown, the piece having often been considered either a gift of Louis XI during his visit in 1473, or a present brought from England by Tanneguy II Le Veneur, sent as ambassador across the Channel to negotiate the marriage of Henriette de France with the future Charles I. Yet the two *écus*, sewn on the back of the chasuble, bear the arms of the Blossets whose last representative, Jean, died in 1531, which might suggest the presence of this vestment at Carrouges before this date.

One hypothesis might be postulated nonetheless. By the late 1400s, Jean and Marie Blosset's brother, Pierre Blosset, called the Monk, was in contact with Marguerite de Luxembourg with whom he had established an exchange of land. Elisabeth Woodville, queen of England, married to Edward IV, was, through her mother, of the Luxembourg line. The chasuble, perhaps offered as a gift to a member of this family, would as such have passed down to Pierre Blosset.

♦ Orphrey (also orfray): a large, woven, embroidered band, highlighted with gold, decorating priestly vestments.

The first Le Veneurs (1450-1550)

The Le Veneurs are represented in the heralds' armorial either under the name Le Veneur, or under that of de Tiliers or Tillières, with variants. The most frequently used blazon is that which has spanned the centuries: "Le Veneur, of silver on an azur band fretted with gold" or "of silver with a band of azur charged with three small gold crosses", as above. Their devise, *Sic sic licet esse beatis*, signifies "Such as it is pleases me".

In 1450, Marie Blosset married Philippe Le Veneur, son of Jean VIII Le Veneur, lord of Home, killed at Azincourt, and of Jeanne Le Baveux, heiress to Tillières (Eure). The two estates of Carrouges and Tillières were thus united under the same head.

The origin of the Le Veneur family dates back to the XIth century: one member was said to have served as the *grand veneur* or master of the royal hounds♦ under William the Conquerer. This responsibility did indeed pass on to Jean, grand master of waters and forests and *veneur* to king Philippe le Bel in 1289. His sons, Robert and Jean, once again became *grands veneurs* de France in 1308 and 1312.

Three of Marie Blosset and Philippe Le Veneur's children became men of the Church, among the most prestigious. Jean was singular in having left a mark on Carrouges. Bishop and comte de Lisieux in 1505 (succeeding his uncle Étienne Blosset), he was the confidant to François I and was called to sit on the

♦ ***Grand veneur:*** *he who commands all the king's game hunting (the art of stag-hunting to horn and hounds).*

The châtelet, or small fortified gatehouse, confined by four towers with steeply pitched, pointed roofs, guards the estate's entrance.

Posthumous portrait of Cardinal Jean Le Veneur, major figure of the Renaissance. Oil on canvas, Château de Carrouges (grand salon), 17th century.

Royal Council. In 1517, he attended the coronation of queen Claude and in 1526, as principal chaplain of France, crowned queen Éléonore. In 1532, he presented Jacques Cartier to the king, contributed to the costs of his expedition to Canada and designated the chaplains of the Mont-Saint-Michel (of which he was the first commendatary abbot) to depart with the navigator. Raised to cardinalship in 1533, he died on 7 August 1543. Amateur of literature, Jean Le Veneur is cited by Rabelais in Book IV of Pantagruel, and Carrouges might have served as one of the models for the Abbey of Thélème.

Jean Le Veneur commissioned for the building of the châtelet which marks the north entry to the estate. Although relatively scaled-down, this edifice was conceived as an independent pavilion on two storeys. If the decorative composition remains Gothic, characterized by pinnacles and elaborate triangulated gables♦ with crockets, the treatment of such elements testifies to a period of artistic transition toward the Renaissance, typical of the first two decades of the 16th century. Black brick ornamentation (which makes up the episcopal crook but not the cardinal's hat) allows one to date the edifice between 1505 and 1533, year in which Jean Le Veneur became cardinal.

♦ ***Gable:*** *a thin wall, more or less moulded or ornamented with openwork, crowning an arch or a bay, frequently used in Gothic architecture.*

Brick décor, black against a red-brick background. The mitre is surrounded by two stylized bishop's crooks.

Jean IX, baron of Tillières and lord of Carrouges, was the son of François, the cardinal's brother. He inherited the château upon the latter's death. He was the king's master of the hounds in 1506, captain of Vire, bailiff of Rouen in 1513, and *pannetier* to queen Éléonore of Austria. In 1510, he wed Gilonne de Montéjean. At Tillières, he had the château and church choir reconstructed, since destroyed. At Carrouges, perhaps it was he who commissioned the small wing linking the ancient donjon with the north-east residential block. As high as the latter, this section was no doubt erected above an old curtain-wall fragment in which an access door to the château was fitted. This cart entrance♦ (a trace of which can still be detected on the exterior, to the left of the donjon) in all likelihood was walled up during the construction of the Blosset wing in the late 15th century. Before 1550, the year of his death, Jean IX also might have had the new door to the staircase tower (framed by two Ionic pilasters) pierced through, abandoning the custom, typical of western France, of reaching the upper floors through a ground-floor room.

♦ ***Cart entrance:*** *door of sufficient size to accommodate the passage of harnessed carriages.*

The Le Veneur ironworks

At the close of the 15th century, but predominantly in the 16th and 17th centuries, Normandy had become the premier iron metallurgy region in the kingdom. In this context, the Le Veneurs, owners of the châteaux de Tillières and de Carrouges, played a particularly outstanding role. Five of them became powerful industrialists. Their considerable forestry inheritance – nearly 3,000 hectares – clearly facilitated the exploitatiown of ironworks. In Normandy and Maine, they alone were at the origin of the birth or renaissance of a dozen iron metallurgy establishments from the late 1400s to the 1630s. It was to this new economic domain and the movement of capital which it implied that the family owed its fortune and the leading role they were to play during the Renaissance and early *Grand Siècle*.

Around 1540, Jean IX Le Veneur, baron of Tillières, lord of Carrouges, created the Carrouges forge. The act of approval dates from 1556. In the 17th century, it was an autonomous establishment comprised of a smelting furnace, refinery and splitting-mill. Constructions established along the banks of the Udon River, in the parishes of Sainte-Marguerite-de-Carrouges and those of Saint-Martin-l'Aiguillon, have almost all disappeared.

In the smelting furnace, the raw mineral became cast iron: one produced pig♦ for the manufacture of iron as well as finished products like firebacks.

At the refinery, the pig was transformed into iron. Hammered into bars, it was then delivered to the splitting-mill.

Iron merchandise was sold to artisans: wrought-iron craftsmen, locksmiths, nailmakers, blacksmiths and the like.

The most spectacular of this production was the ceremonial wrought-iron work still in place, in part, in the park of the château. The grand gateway and its surrounding railing, the south gate, that of La Bouvardière, and the colonnade were all crafted – as attested by notarized certificates – with iron produced locally.

Between 1641 and 1648 Jacques Le Veneur placed several orders with Issac Geslin, marshal of the parish of Sainte-Marguerite-de-Carrouges, to execute works after the drawings of Jacques Groisil, under the direction of architect Maurice Gabriel from Argentan.

Operated with uneven success, the Carrouges forge remained active until 1854.

♦ **Pig:** *crude iron bar obtained direct from smelting furnaces.*

Monogram of Issac Geslin (Alençon, Office of the Archives départementales de l'Orne).

Splendour of the Le Veneurs (1550-1653)

Gabriel, Jean IX's eldest son, succeeded his great-uncle Ambroise as bishop of Évreux. He was abbot of Saint-Taurin d'Évreux, Lyre, Saint-Évroult and Jumièges. Machiavelli dedicated one of his works to him. He ceded Carrouges to his younger brother Tanneguy I, first comte de Tillières (the Tillières lands were established as a county in 1565). The latter was governor of the province, bailiff and governor of Rouen. At the château, he received Catherine de Medicis and her retenue in 1570. Brantôme spoke of the freedom of his exchanges with the queen, whilst Thou, Sully and Agrippa d'Aubigné noted his tolerant character, as attested by his attitude during the Saint Bartholomew's Day Massacre which he attempted to prevent in Rouen. In 1582 he was made knight of Saint-Esprit.

Wing of the grand apartments.

Gabriel Le Veneur died in 1591 before having received the royal warrant of marshal promised him by king Henri III in 1588. It was likely around 1575 that Tanneguy I initiated an ambitious building programme which would give new scale to the dwelling. The south-west and south-east wings, respectively called "the gallery wing", and "grand apartments", were then entirely built. The court façade of the Blosset wing was itself recast to harmonize with the new ensemble. Two monumental staircases (completed in 1579), constituting the architectural jewels of this construction phase, were erected to face one another at the east and south corners of the court. Their design concept radically broke with the spirals which until then served the upper storeys.

The project of the lord of Carrouges undoubtedly underlined a desire to augment and reorganize the château, without simultaneously destroying the old residence. In the east corner of the château, the liaison between the extremity of the Gothic central block and the 16th-century wing proved to be particularly complex. The smallest of the two new staircases was constructed within the continuity of the old block, whilst the new wing was extended to the pentagonal tower, with its probably ancient foundations, encompassing the angle of the oblique pavilion. What resulted was a minuscule, invisible triangular court (called the "prison court"). Overlooking the moats, the junction between the pentagonal tower, the late 15th-century pavilion and the 16th-century wing is hardly elegant.

Very shortly before the construction of these new dwellings, the foundations of a large, bastioned pavilion set obliquely to the west of the court had been laid down, perhaps on the emplacement of an ancient angled tower. The first level of this bastion adopted the idea of an old keep with a central room protected by a corridor leading to a shooting chamber. With its exclusively defensive character, this construction contrasts with the slightly later new wings. Perhaps dictated by the ephemeral anxieties of the owners of Carrouges in the troubled climate of the Wars of Religion, this pavilion housed a kitchen until 1787 (today called "the bakery"), whilst the upper floor, modified in the late 18th century, housed the Pompadour salon. No doubt in the same way as the presence of the ancient curtain-walls on which the new constructions bore down, the salon's position reinforced the asymmetry of the plan, already weighed down by the presence of the Medieval abodes.

It is not known whether the Argentan architect François Gabriel — ancestor to the celebrated dynasty of builders and whose participation in the enlargement of Carrouges is the first confirmed construction work – had conceived a design proposal. He can be credited with the careful unification of the château's disparate elements so as to render their heterogeneity less perceptible. At Carrouges, the architect manifested a taste for a declared Classical sobriety which one rediscovers in projects of a later period, such as at Fervaques (Calvados).

Such rigour is visible foremost within the interior court where the same slightly projecting granite band emphasizes each level and demarcates the window bays which open at irregular intervals along the stretch of blind masonry walls. The lozenges or black-brick chevron motifs, the cornice with modillions♦ and the identical dormer windows successfully unify the various wings.

♦ ***Modillion:*** *small projecting supports or brackets, most often cubic, running at close intervals beneath a cornice.*

As in the old Medieval dwellings, the lower level was allotted to service zones (cellars, reserves, stables, kitchens, muckrooms and the like), whilst the noble apartments occupied the upper level. Attics were reserved for bed- and linen rooms.

Tanneguy I Le Veneur's successors contented themselves with modifying the interior arrangements of their residence and gardens. The edifice existed much as one sees it today.

From his marriage with Madeleine de Pompadour, Tanneguy I produced three children of whom Jacques, the second comte de Tillières, inherited his father's responsibilities at Rouen. Tanneguy I was driven out of the city at the news of the assassination of the duc de Guise (1586). Henri IV (whom he had

The wing of the gallery, abutting to the left against the bastion, overlooks the terraced gardens and vast pond, drained by General Le Veneur in the late 1700s.

perhaps received at the château de Carrouges) benefited from his support. He died in 1595. His sister Marie married Paul de Salm, grand chamberlain to the duc de Lorraine and baron de Brandebourg. Their descendants were distinguished. Tanneguy II, eldest of Jacques Le Veneur and Charlotte Chabot's children,

Marie Le Veneur. This frail young woman, married to the comte de Salm, was the mother to Christine, duchesse de Lorraine, whose descendants established the Hapsburg-Lorraine dynasty which (after the War of Succession of Austria) reigned over the Austro-Hungarian Empire until Otto of Hapsburg's renunciation of the throne in 1961. Marie-Antoinette of Austria, queen of France in 1770, and Marie-Louise, empress of the French people in 1810, both descended from Marie Le Veneur. The notice painted on her portrait, composed by the General, describes her as the "sixth grandmother of the reigning Emperor". This refers to François II, emperor from 1792-1855, father of seven children of which the eldest, Marie-Louise, was the wife of Napoleon. Oil on canvas, Château de Carrouges (ceremonial antechamber).

was councillor to the king. In 1608 he wed Catherine de Bassompierre, sister of the marshal of France. In 1619, Louis III dispatched him to England on a mission to negotiate the marriage of Henriette de France, his sister, with the future king Charles I, concluded in 1625. Upon his return to France after nine years' absence, Tanneguy II suffered from the disgrace of his brother-in-law Bassompierre and lived on his lands at Tillières. In 1634, he legated Carrouges to his brother Jacques, commendatary abbot of Silly-en-Gouffern, who had already assumed building works there. The estate's physiognomy, from park to apartments, was modified, construction enduring until the death of the master in 1653. In the park, the gardens were redesigned; a major network of walls, balustrades and grilles emphasized the paths and demarcated the lower court and the terrace.

The Gabriels at Carrouges

The first representatives of this illustrious dynasty of architects began to practice their trade around Argentan (Orne region) as far back as the late 16th century.

The name of François Gabriel, the eldest of this lineage, appeared for the first time in the accounts register established for the years 1578 to 1582, at the time when the two new wings of the château of Carrouges were being completed. He was next called to Torigni-sur-Vire (Manche region) by the marshal of Matignon, and in 1588 completed the staircase of the nearby château de Canisy. His renown also earned him the direction of construction at the château de Fervaques (Calvados) in 1599 where the Classical severity of his style, already perceptible at Carrouges, was freed from his Mannerist experiments executed for the Matignons.

François' son Jacques I Gabriel was principally active around Argentan, Caen and Rouen. It was to Maurice (chief architect of the clock-tower at the Church of Saint-Germain d'Argentan) that the task of pursuing his grandfather's work at Carrouges reverted. Receiving the château in 1634, Jacques Le Veneur established a construction site which lasted until his death in 1653. Maurice Gabriel was first commissioned to refurbish the gardens whose balustrades and grilles were set in place after his plans. In 1642 he was in charge of the family chapel décor in the church of the canonical community. There the architect accomplished mainly ornamental work, which, in 1648 (a year before his death), he carried on at the château itself by directing the execution of the wainscotting of the 'ceiling chamber' (now the bishops' chamber).

Maurice's son Jacques III Gabriel was the first to establish a career in Paris, preparing the success of his descendants, designers of the city hall in Rennes, the Place Vendôme in Paris, and the Petit Trianon and Opéra at Versailles.

Central well-hole of the ceremonial staircase, by François Gabriel (low angle shot). The painted plaster which covered the bricks enhanced the sober geometry of this staircase which leads to the "grand apartments" and the gallery.

Some boxwood was planted and fifty "leaden" earthenware pots (covered with green or yellow plombiferous glazing) purchased in Alençon. Like his ancestor, Jacques Le Veneur called on the Gabriels: Maurice, grandson of François, was the author of the new arrangement of the gardens. He designed and supervised the décor of the familial funerary chapel at the Collegiate of Notre-Dame-de-Bon-Confort in 1642. Maurice was also the designer of some, if not the totality, of the château's wainscotting decoration, such as the 'ceiling chamber' (now the bishops' chamber, closed for restoration) and the sculpted-wood motifs decorating the beams of the ceremonial antechamber, commissioned in 1649. The old timber ceiling with beams "as full as empty" is embellished by a painted canvas to imitate caissons, whilst the Gothic chimney, modified and decorated with 16th-century frescoes, was masked by wainscotting decoration, since dismantled. Louis XI's chamber (harbouring the memory of the king's visit to the château in 1473) was refurbished in the same era.

A minuscule oratory, with richly decorated coffered ceiling and ornate panelling of sculpted motifs and paintings, adjoins the bishop's chamber.

The inventory compiled on 24 October 1653 after Jacques Le Veneur's death attests to the wealth of furniture, pictures and objects (such as silver service) and to their location. Description of the gallery (currently the festival hall) confirms the taste of a true art lover with the presence, among family portraits, of many tableaux, the majority since dispersed, by renowned artists such as Albani, Guido Reni and Guerchino, commissioned during the prelate's Italian sojourns. In 1609, his sister Anne, lady-in-waiting to Madame, duchesse d'Orléans, governess to Mademoiselle, married François de Fiesque, comte de Lavagne and de Bressuire, member of an illustrious Genoese family.

Décor with fenestrated wainscotting in Louis XI's chamber.

Disgrace and renewal (1653-1777)

In 1638 Henry Le Veneur, Tanneguy II's son, the ambassador, wed Claude Rouault. He lived on a grand scale, yet founded a charitable brotherhood which he generously endowed. Works he undertook were restricted to his farms and iron foundry. He died in 1687, leaving three children, among them François (1641-1687), heir to Carrouges, who married Anne Favier du Boulay, daughter of the intendant d'Alençon. Still suffering the effects of Tanneguy II's disgrace, these two generations were distanced from court responsibilities. They effected neither transformations nor embellishments to the château.
It was with Tanneguy III (1671-1748) that the family recovered public respect and contracted prestigious alliances once again. Colonel of the Cravattes-Cavalerie regiment, he was named brigadier of the king's army in 1703. In 1699, he married Michelle Gabrielle du Gué de Bagnols, daughter to the state councillor Louis Dreux du Gué. Close relative to Louvois, she was the niece of Madame de Coulanges, celebrated wit and literary figure. Her uncle de

These boundary stones, still visible along the edge of Écouves forest, were set in place at the very start of the 17th century. They indicate the separation between crown lands and the woods of Goult just purchased by Jacques Le Veneur from the Montgommerys. *Recto*, the *fleur-de-lys* of the royal domain; *verso*, the Le Veneur arms.

Opposite
The châtelet, a view by Émile Sagot. Lithograph, circa 1850.

Anne Gabrielle and Jacques Tanneguy IV, as children, one of the rare portraits at Carrouges on view and the sole depiction of the Le Veneur children. Oil on canvas, early 18th century. Château de Carrouges (grand salon).

Coulanges was himself Madame de Sévigné's cousin. Their portraits are in the château collection. Tanneguy III did not make major changes to his properties. Nonetheless, sincerely wanting to administer them to the best, he commissioned a plan of the Carrouges estate to be drawn up in 1711. It constitutes a precious document on the condition of the château, park and gardens at this period. The couple's children were Anne Gabrielle (1699-1777) and Jacques Tanneguy IV (1700-1777) who successfully pursued a military career. Brigadier, he was obliged to quit the army following the disgrace of his brother-in-law, the duc de Châtillon, his sister's second husband.
Tanneguy IV's wife, Michelle Bouchard d'Esparbès de Lussan d'Aubeterre de Jonzac, was the niece of president Hénault, academician and superintendent to queen Marie Leszczinska. He divided his time between his Parisian mansion and the Château de Tillières where it appears that he refurbished the furniture.
François Jacques Tanneguy V (1739-1811), his eldest son, inherited Tillières. Carrouges went to Alexis Paul Michel, vicomte Le Veneur, a man above the ordinary.

The brick

From the start of construction at the end of the 14th century, the choice of brick was due to the presence of clay as raw material on the site. One was obliged to bring granite, difficult to extract and harder to cut, from a dozen kilometres afar. Clay brick had to be left to rot in winter, then put into moulds and baked in stacks with charcoal and wood. According to the ambient temperature and firing conditions, tones ranged from pale pink to deep black. During the Middle Ages, all these nuances were mixed without distinction. By the Renaissance, black bricks enlivened the façade through a clever geometry of various shapes. Ubiquitous in Normandy, this fashion was invented at Carrouges with the construction of the châtelet.
A brick-coloured plaster coat with a configuration of white joints often covered authentic masonry bond, inside as well as outside, rendering it more agreeable to the eye.

Plain bond.

Lozenge-shaped bond.

False brick sections.

The chairs at Carrouges

This Louis-XV fauteuil, covered in petit-point tapestry, with a wide, deep and very low seat, called a "*marquise*" allows ladies to sit comfortably despite their ample dresses. Château de Carrouges (grand salon).

In 1936, along with the château, the state purchased the majority of its furniture including one hundred and fifty chairs, for the most part presently furnishing the rooms open to the public. From Louis XI's chamber to the grand salon, 17th- to 19th-century styles are represented.

There were always a quantity of chairs at Carrouges: inheritances, divisions, rejects and successive contributions translated into an ensemble that well preserves the living history of a provincial château during its splendrous moments.

The inventory written at the death of Jacques Le Veneur on 24 October 1653 included one hundred and ninety-seven "*fauteulx, sièges pliants ou ployants, chesses*" [arm-, folding or bent and straight-backed chairs].

The château furniture inventoried by General Le Veneur on 1 November 1822 numbered three hundred and forty-three chairs. Their description was highly detailed: fabric upholstery included velour from Utrecht, tapestry and silk, Indian cotton, "*jouie*" [Jouay] cotton toile, moquette, damask and woollen cloth. Colours varied: yellow, blue, red, violet, green, green-and-white or red-and-white check and mauve, among other shades.

Refurbishment during the 1950s limited the chair upholstery in the grand apartment to plain or embossed red velours. The last restoration, undertaken in 1994, made a selection of ten different coverings using fabrics, colours and designs in keeping with the style of chairs and in harmony with the wall decorations.

Stamp (woodworker's signature) of Jean-Baptiste Lelarge (1711-1771), master in 1738, on an armchair in the grand salon.

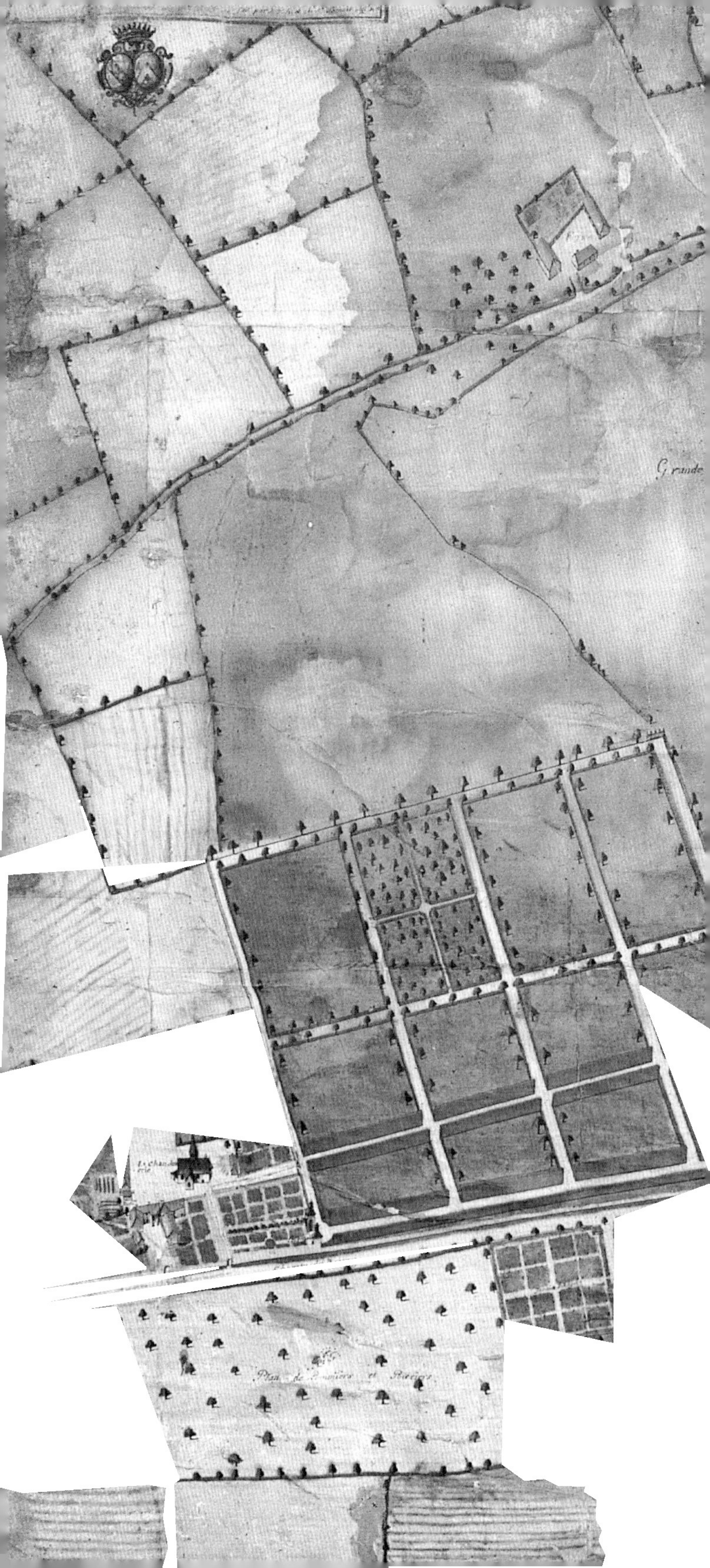
Grande

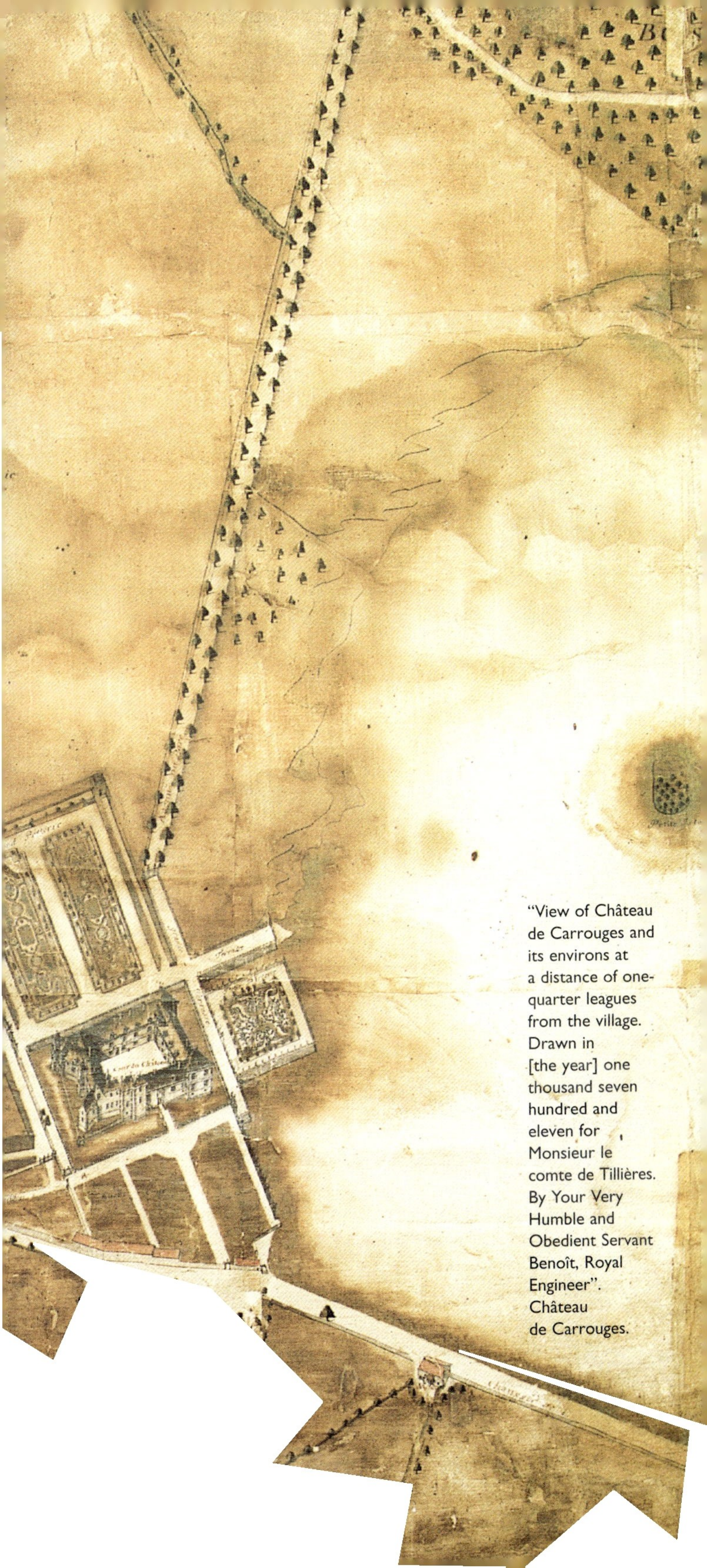

"View of Château de Carrouges and its environs at a distance of one-quarter leagues from the village. Drawn in [the year] one thousand seven hundred and eleven for Monsieur le comte de Tillières. By Your Very Humble and Obedient Servant Benoît, Royal Engineer". Château de Carrouges.

General Le Veneur and his descendants

(1777-1936)

Alexis Paul Michel Le Veneur, general of the division. Under the Restoration, he wore the cross of Saint-Louis which he had recently received, along with the Legion of Honour awarded by Napoleon I. Oil on canvas, circa 1830. Château de Carrouges (coll. CMN).

Youngest of the family, vicomte Alexis Le Veneur chose, like many others, a military career. Born under Louis XV and died under Louis-Philippe, he traversed the end of the Old Regime, the first Republic, the first Empire and the Restoration. As a free mason, he espoused new ideas and welcomed the Revolution in which he enthusiastically participated. Almost the victim of his zeal, he was compromised by the treasons of Dumouriez and La Fayette and was imprisoned. First mayor of the commune of Carrouges and president of the General Council of the department of Orne, he was honoured by Napoleon who elected him *comte d'Empire avec majorat* [title of nobility transmitted to the eldest son]. His name is engraved on the vault of the Arc de Triomphe de l'Étoile in Paris. At the château, he transformed the ancient drawbridge, replaced by a Louis-XV entry with fixed bridge. To create a festival hall intended for theatre, music and balls, he did not hesitate to eliminate the second floor of the gallery wing (south-west block).

Perhaps he even considered razing the old dwelling to replace it with a more fashionably styled château. He had intended to transform the Blosset wing facing the moats as the principal façade in the direction of the village. The project involved the construction of a monumental bridge with steps and landings above the moat, leading up to a new entrance. As part of his construction plan, or as an act of public spiritedness, he had the tower of the chapel demolished, without pursuing his building works. The pond was drained and numerous projects to redesign the gardens established to create a landscaped park. The archives

Life at Carrouges
at the time of General Le Veneur.

Among family members, the custom was to perform in comedies or small operas. Balls were frequent. One of the children played the flute, the general composed tender rhyming songs. These activities accommodated themselves with difficulty to the noisy kitchen service. So that from then on meals were prepared in the 15th-century wing. The dining-room was definitively established on the upper floor in one of the more commodious halls. The general kept a very meticulous inventory of volumes comprising his library "rich among the provincial libraries". Works on geography, voyage accounts, treatises on tactics and political books kept company with the complete set of the *Encyclopédie*. Racine and Corneille figured there alongside Rousseau and Voltaire.

A correspondence which Victor de Novilar (come alone to Carrouges to wed Aménaïde Henriette Louise Le Veneur in 1808) addressed to his father conveys a fine impression of the way of life at the house: "We were thirty-two at table this evening and the dining-room could have held double that number. The billiards room which serves as a hall for entertainment is almost as grand, without including the theatre [...]. One eats luncheon with a fork, everyone reunited in the salon" (1 April). "I had occasion to judge the kind of order that reigned in the house. A businessman for the control of rural properties, [and] surveillance of the château and persons in the absence of M[onsieur] le Veneur, lives in the detached pavilion at the château. A male domestic for Monsieur, a female cook and baker at the oven every day, one for washing, five chambermaids, a girl for the daughter-in-law's children, all these women sewing in the same chamber under the inspection of an old nursery nurse, as soon as the service of the house was done, three or four women labourers, such were the regular inhabitants of the house, then the concierge to carry and deliver letters to the village of Carrourges, clean the courtyards, two old invalids who transport wood and water to all parts of the château. The bell rings regularly for breakfast at nine o'clock, at one o'clock rings the setting of table, at one-thirty the dinner, at nine o'clock and nine-thirty the supper. Almost daily we had hares, rabbits and seafood which one was obliged to go find on the Caen-Paris route seven leagues from here..." (14 April).

Madame de Verdelin, here represented with her daughters, was the benefactress of Jean-Jacques Rousseau and the mother-in-law of the general. Pastel, Château de Carrouges (summer salon), second-half of the 18th century.

are full of notebooks filled with his condensed, methodical handwritten dictation of his orders for estate management. To facilitate comprehension, he established an enumeration of chambers, rooms and salons. The residence was enriched in 1823 with objects from the Château de Tillières before it was bought and destroyed by the "black band"♦.

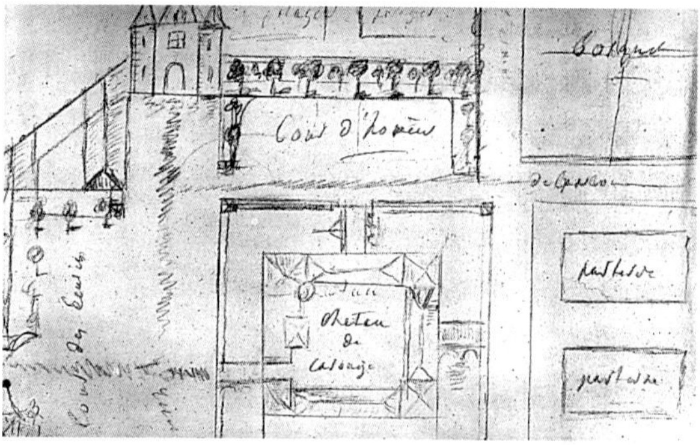

One of numerous sketches drawn by the General describing his proposals for the reorganization of the park. Here figure two new bridges; only the one near the parterres was executed, still in place at the beginning of the 20th century.

At the death of the General, it was Alexis Louis Jacques Tanneguy VI (1779-1851) who inherited Carrouges. He participated in the life of the department as councillor-general and wed Alexandrine Bibienne Félicité de Jupilles, great grandaughter, by her mother, of the marquis de Torcy-Colbert. Their six children and their families lived at the château which incurred a good number of interior modifications, such as the installation of very small chambers in the attics. The eldest, Alexandre Charles Michel Tanneguy VII (1806-1856) and his wife Marie Amélie de Bertier made some transformations in the wing of the grand apartments, giving the grand salon its actual proportions. They had six daughters and one son.
This last, Marie Joseph Ambroise Tanneguy VIII (1851-1925), married Anne Marie Amélie de Preaulx. Their three children constituted the last generation of Le Veneurs.
Marie Gaston Tanneguy IX, born in 1882, was the last owner of Carrouges. In 1936, at fifty-four years old, not having a descendant and not being able to face the heavy expenses incurred by such a vast dwelling, he found himself obliged to put the château up for sale.

♦ ***Black band:*** *the "black band", created under the Restoration, was an association of speculators who bought up grand properties and "venerable" monuments to parcellate and demolish them and resell the building materials.*

Sketch by Godard, on a visit to Carrouges, circa 1830 (Bibliothèque d'Alençon).

The legend of Carrouges

Hunting scene. Fresco, Château de Carrouges (chimneypiece in the ceremonial antechamber), 16th century.

In the popular imagination, the existence of the château was confirmed from the 6th century, in the Merovingian age, by a terrible story wherein the supernatural mixes with a betrayal of love, spilt blood and a hereditary curse.

Évelyne du Champ de la Pierre married Ralph, sire de Carrouges. An heir to the name and estate was very long awaited. When the lady finally felt herself to be carrying the hope of her husband, a sumptuous fête was organized, enduring for seven days.

A hunt of wild beasts in the immense neighbouring forest crowned the jubilations. By evening, the count did not return to his dwelling. He had encountered a fairy with incomparable traits, reflecting her charms in the waters of a source illuminated by the golden moon. Every night his faithful horse led Ralph to enduring bliss at the fountain's edge.

By guile, one moonlit night, his wife discovered the object of his betrayal. She armed herself with a gold dagger, slayed her rival and returned to take to bed, smitten with strange pains. In the morning, Ralph's bloodstained body lay in the château courtyard, its heart pierced with the fatal knife. The countess, alerted, gave birth to a son and died bloodless without having ever recognized him.

The new-born orphan was red-headed. He bore a large bloodstain on his forehead which never healed. He was baptized Karl-the-Red or Carouge, from hence derived the name of this red-brick château. And during seven generations, all the Carrouges were red-heads and marked by a stain of shame on their forehead. Male descendants would never again follow: the house fell to the distaff side♦.

The text of this legend was published for the first time in the mid-19th century by Edmond de Manne, keeper at the Bibliothèque nationale. With the tale of the judicial duel of the last Carrouges, it attracted the attention of Alexandre Dumas (see p.9).

The families allied to Carrouges – the Carrouges and their lily on a "field of red", the Blossets and their "chevrons on watered red" on their blazon, the Le Veneurs and their "little gold crosses" – were extinct families, without male descendants. Troubling legend ....

♦ ***To fall to the distaff side:*** *said of a family with no male descendants.*

A national monument (since 1936)

From 1927, the State classified the Château de Carrouges as an historic monument. This protection intervened at a crucial moment for the estate: terraces and gardens lay abandoned; roofs were beginning to leak; struts propped up the heavy beams within the apartments.

The château was put up for sale by adjudication on 5 March 1936 for a sum of 300,000 francs. As no purchaser appeared, a second offer was made on 23 April for 200,000 francs. Slightly by chance, the State bought it .... Reserving a portion of the movables (furniture and portraits), the Administration sought to maintain the living character of this superior dwelling. Other than a few recent certified copies of pieces at the château, and the tapestries acquired in 1986, the ensemble of furniture and portraits belonged to the Le Veneur family.

In January 1937, an important auction sale took place during ten days which dispersed the silverware, china, linen, furniture and objects. Very rapidly, conservation measures were undertaken regarding the building, notably water protection. It was necessary to wait until 1978 for the entire roof complex to be completely restored.

From 1938, estimates were established to restore the furniture. In September 1939, the château was in sufficiently good condition to receive collections salvaged from museums in Rouen (ceramics, precious books) along with highly valuable stained glass and objects from other provenances. Its isolated position and the fact that it was off bounds to troops made it a safe place. Nonetheless the domain suffered from the battles of the Liberation. On Sunday, 13 August 1944, some German soldiers took refuge with a munitions vehicle, under the châtelet entrance. Upon the arrival of the American liberators, they opened fire. The riposte provoked a fire in the vehicle and inevitably spread to the châtelet.

Major restoration work began in the 1950s. Movables were restored under successive campaigns. Structural work intervened in the outbuildings and the park as well. Balustrades were consolidated; the moats were refilled in the 1960s.

Detail of the tapestry *Abraham and the Three Strangers* by Sébastien de la Planche: Sarah, wife of Abraham. Château de Carrouges (dining-room), mid-17th century.

Romantic view of the château before 1927. Won over by physiocrats who advocated increasing the area of productive lands, the General had the moats and pond drained. The former was fitted with an access ramp permitting cattle to graze there.

A study is now underway to rehabilitate the park and its gardens, the objective being to approximate the 17th-century condition as described in the plan of 1711.

Maintained since 1995 by the *Centre des monuments nationaux* (formerly *Caisse nationale des monuments historiques et des sites*), the estate is open to visitors 360 days per year. It accommodates cultural events (concerts, exhibitions, activities) from spring to autumn, as well as festivities in the park.

War wounds (Sunday, 13 August 1944).

Following double page
Châtelet and château in February 1994.

CHATEAU
VISITEURS

Visit

Along the moats

Only a promenade along the moats allows one to appreciate the true measure of the building and its 300-metres façade, enclosing a court undetectable from the exterior. It is crowned by a continuous slate roof of around one hectare.
The homogeneous appearance (due to the uniform use of brick materials) is contradicted by certain architectural details and a few complex interweavings which reveal contributions of various construction campaigns.
To get the best impression, while heading toward the châtelet from the bridge, one should stop at the north corner of the moat.
There unfolds the two most ancient façades. The one, to the right, encompasses the donjon towers recognizable by their machicolations, flanked in the foreground by a small 16th-century wing and, to the rear, the bastion.
The other, to the left, the Blosset wing, is composed of a main block and oblique pavilions with their dormers topped by pointed pediments.
On the façade, some masonry repairs mark out the emplacement of a chapel destroyed by the General.
At the end of the 18th century, the ramp was designed to access both the drained moat and the pond.
To the rear, a small defensive tower retains its loop holes in the lower ranges and, in the upper parts, traces of plaster from the late 17th century.
Continuing along the visitor sees unfolding the south-east wing (called the grand apartments).
Rising above the ancient foundations (several times recast) where little accoladed openings have been preserved, the wing is punctuated by granite bands and wide bay perforations.
Three white limestones would have borne the family arms associated with the château; they were hacked away during the Revolution. Beyond the south pavilion, overlooking the terraced garden, extends the gallery wing, adjoining the west bastion, constructed on a spur, and offering the same consistent simplicity.
On the return, facing the bridge, one notices the large opening created in the 18th century to illuminate the Pompadour salon. The drawbridge still existed in 1808. It was transformed into a fixed bridge by the General, its entry crowned by a Classical pediment. A granite balustrade ornamented with openwork outlines the moat fed by fresh spring water.

The Blosset wing, to the right, the grand apartment wings, to the left, from one end to the other of the east defensive tower.

The interior court

♦ ***Mullion:***
stone jamb, sometimes moulded, vertically dividing a bay.

♦ ***Transom (cross bar):***
stone element horizontally partitioning a bay. Transom windows (often combined with a jamb) were utilized from mid-14th- to mid-17th-century.

Appearing more homogeneous than the château exteriors, the court nonetheless bears witness to different phases of its constitution. The donjon clearly stands out by its mass and disjuncture with the relative symmetry of this enclosed space. At the south corner, one perceives once again traces of a staircase turret which served the upper floors.
The small wing constructed against it in the 16th century has recovered its mullions♦ and transoms♦ at the windows, no doubt destroyed in the late 18th century when modern frames were installed.
Only three Gothic elements — the restored ogival door (opening to the guards room), the staircase tower, as well as the Gothic chimney stack — signal the Medieval origins of the Blosset wing whose façade was altered during construction of the château's new wings.
Those latter wings occupy nearly three sides of the court and bear the same ornamentation of black-brick chevrons and lozanges running between the red bricks, and by granite bands indicating the floor levels and underlining the window bays. Particularly sober, the rigourous ordinance of their façaces does not allow speculation over the function of interior spaces. Only the twin dormers surmounted by clerestories indicate the presence of two monumental staircases constructed at either end of the court.

The donjon

The donjon is sole evidence of the ancient, late 14th-century fortified château. Undoubtedly the constituent part of an entire military and residential ensemble, it was nevertheless conceived to be independently autodefensive thanks to its machicolations which protected it from attacks coming either from the exterior or the court. The ground floor (simultaneously guards room and kitchen) could, when needed, be transformed into a veritable mousetrap: an assailant who managed to slip in there exposed himself to firing from the shooting gallery within the west square turret, as well as from the corridor (pierced by an arrow slit♦) which linked it with the stair tower opposite, since destroyed.

A well, hollowed out within one of the window embrasures, provided a water supply, eliminating the need to go into the courtyard. The second bay facing the court retains its window seat♦. An old pivoting measure evokes the policing of markets and fairs exercised by the lords of Carrouges.

As on the first floor (closed to visitors), the second floor was occupied by a bed-chamber completed by a *garde-robe* equipped with latrines.

Later constructions flanking the donjon did not necessitate the suppression of the machicolations which, now redundant, ornament the renovated room interiors, used for temporary exhibitions.

Detail of the machicolations of the donjon.

♦ ***Arrow slit:*** *vertical vent for bow and arrow.*

♦ ***Window seat:*** *stone seat fitted into a window embrasure.*

Ground plan

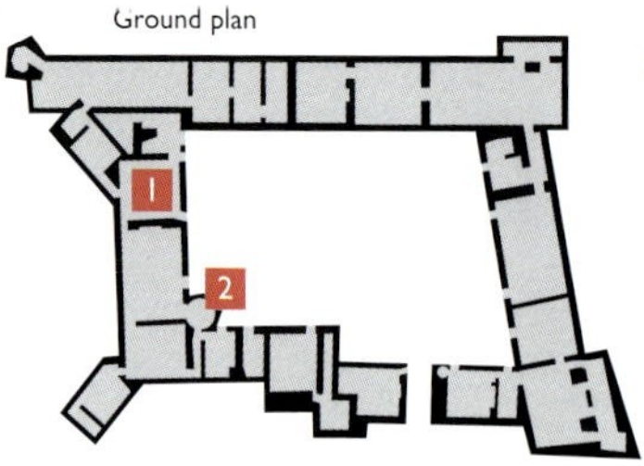

1st floor

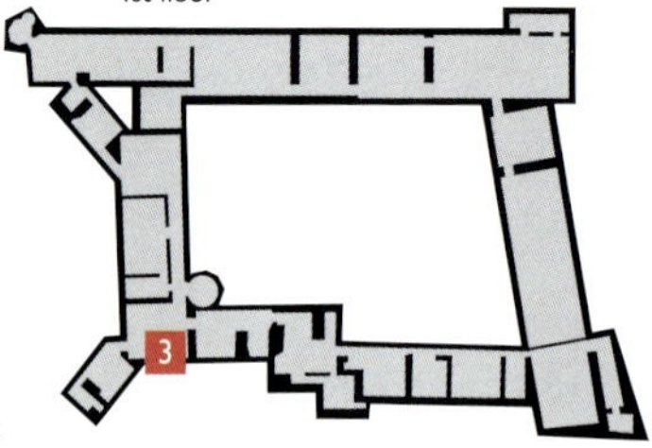

1

The kitchens

It was in the Blosset wing that the kitchens were installed, likely by the end of the 18th century. From the east staircase (which communicates with the kitchens), one reaches the dining-room installed by the General at the same period. The principal room (the only one open to visitors) is extended by a rear-kitchen with chimneypiece and stone sink, and by a cubbyhole which occupies the end of the oblique pavilion. It might be that the window embrasure facing the court had housed a "*potager*", a sort of oven in which one could simmer meat stews and conserves. During the course of the 19th century, the chimney uprights — whose proportions and mouldings on the hood attest to their age – were mutilated to accommodate the installation of a stove. Numerous copperware utensils, in part from the 18th century, were used for cooking meats and fish, jams and sweets. Through the rear door to the left, one reached the staff dining-room which occupied two-thirds of the guards room (the partition having been removed to restore the original volume to this room). During the General's era at the beginning of the 19th century, around twenty persons made up the daily staff at the château. The inventory drawn up upon the death of the General's son in 1851 makes mention of other premises situated on the ground floor which complemented the kitchens: a fruit greenhouse, a pantry with its meat block and hook, a bakery and flour storage, a chicken coop with fowl cages, several wine cellars and so forth.

2

Tower of the charter room

From the court, one mounts the spiral staircase in the Blosset block (which also serves the right-angled, occupied wing) to the second floor, through the temporary exhibition rooms. Originally the three rooms – which occupied the first floor of the main block – were disposed *en enfilade*. One passed from one to the other through small doors situated facing the moats. They were the focus of sumptuous refurbishments in the mid-1600s, commissioned by Jacques Le Veneur, abbot of Silly. Artisans intervened under the direction of "Master Maurice Gabriel, architect", all of them hired locally. The General had a corridor installed (it still cuts through the north salon) to facilitate the arrangement of the three rooms.

3

Louis XI's bed-chamber

Its name evokes the king's visit on 11 August 1473, on his pilgrimage to the Mont-Saint-Michel. Its present décor was installed in the mid-17th century. The imposing 15th-century chimneypiece is dissimulated by a frame of polychrome-and-gilt sculpted wood, very typical of the 1650s. The granite double string course of the Medieval dwelling block (still visible in the kitchens and guards room as well as in the ceremonial antechamber) is painted; it acts as the liaison between the décor of the panelled walls and the ceiling. Two windows light this room. The interior shutters were dismantled so that the visitor might appreciate the refined quality of the decorated embrasures: charming personages, chubby-cheeked cupids and foliage painted *en camaïeu* on small-panelled woodwork. This décor contrasts with the wainscotting panels (perhaps recycled), ornamented with foliage and laurel leaves, which cover the walls. The 17th-century furnishings – tables, stools, chairs – are completed by a chest and canopied bed *à pentes*♦, garnished with a fabric of alternating stripes of velvet and imitation chevroned tapestry. They are reproductions of furniture described in this room. A curious parquet in panels, called "*en échelle*" [laddered], contributes to the comforts.

♦ ***À pentes:*** *bed with curtains all around.*

The décor of the 17th century still survives in this postcar from the 1910s. The date of its dismantling is unknown.

4

The north salon

Upon leaving Louis XI's bed-chamber, one follows the corridor to reach the north salon which occupies the centre of the Blosset wing. In the original concept of the main block, it was a sort of antechamber which also functioned as a vestibule to the chapel.
The wide, accoladed bay gave access to it.
The chapel entry, the small door and its granite frame as well as the immense chinmneypiece (which has not been transformed) testify to the sobriety of the Medieval dwelling. All the same, the room has lost its vast original proportions due to the creation of the corridor and wall partition opposite the hearth to accommodate the *garde-robe* necessary for its use as a bed-chamber. After the last restoration carried out in the 1980s, female portraits (Le Veneur women or close relatives) were reunited here. Like most of the furniture presented in the rooms, the family portraits were acquired by the State in 1936 at the same time as the château. The 18th-century movables (chairs, commodes, Turkish bed) soften the severity of the architectural elements. Terra-cotta tiling covers the floor.
In leaving this room, one continues along the corridor to reach the ceremonial antechamber.

Dressing-*cum*-writing table
"*à dessus brisé*" [with hollow underportion], late 18th century.

5

Ceremonial antechamber

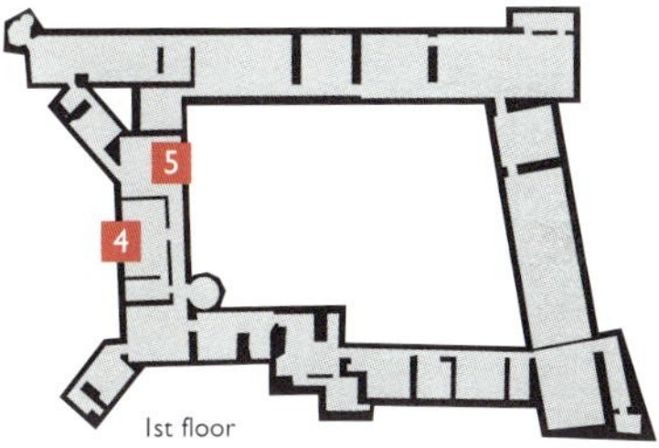

This "chamber at the end of the room" marks the limit of the 15th-century construction. The opening facing the court (link to the east landing) was pierced when the staircase was created, completed in 1579. Simultaneously austere and warm, it is very characteristic of the history of Carrouges. Originally more open, the fireplace dates from the 15th century. On the hood is painted a lively hunting scene. The dress of the personages suggests a 16th-century dating. Later, a lintel decorated with foliage was added to close the hearth; modified uprights gave it more depth.
By mid-17th century, the room was sumptuous: at that time a décor of painted stars (only a few elements remain) and sculpted motifs (still in place) applied on the beams transformed the ceiling. A notarial deed allows us to secure the date, 1649, for commissioning the cartouches of carved wood. As in Louis XI's bed-chamber, the granite string course (visible in each corner of the fireplace and on the wall opposite) was painted, whilst the chimneypiece must have been finished with a carved wood coffer. The ensemble carried the Le Veneur colours: silver (white), azur, gold.
One might suppose that the walls, covered with a plaster coat painted with illusionistic sections of brick, were once furnished with wainscotting or wall-hangings. The tapestry representing Jacob at the well was part of a tripartite hanging acquired in 1986. It bears the mark of Sébastien de la Planche, director of the Parisian Faubourg Saint-Germain workshop in the mid-1600s.
The Renaissance chests, Louis-XIII table and chairs and Louis-XIV armoire animate this handsome room whose floor is garnished with hexagonal terra-cotta pavers. The chimney plaque, dated 1742, is a reminder that the Le Veneurs owned the ironworks.

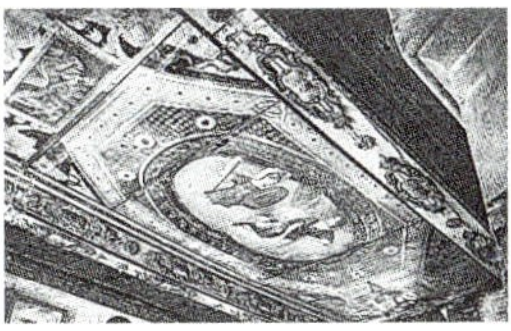

The ceiling of painted canvas is still in place on this postcard from the 1910s.

6

East staircase

Adjacent to the Blosset wing, the staircase maintains the junction between the old Medieval blocks and the new wings of the château. In 1579, date of its completion, this staircase was a novel and audacious concept, contrasting sharply with the narrow turrets containing spiral staircases which served the donjon and Blosset wing. It is entirely built in brick, the single flight revolving around an open central well.

♦ ***Stereotomy:*** *art of designing and cutting stone or brick, in order to be assembled.*

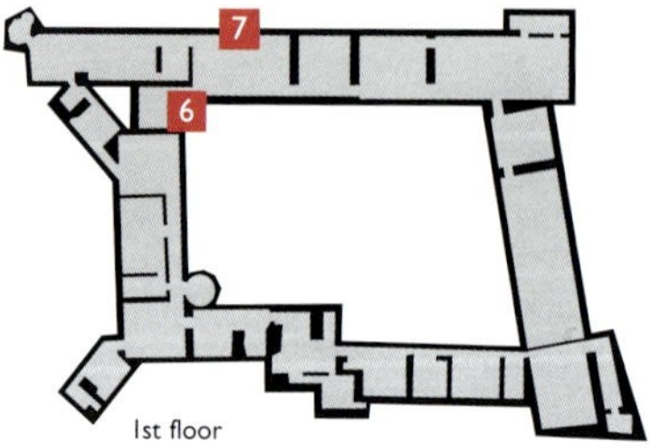

1st floor

The springers of the vaults, which carry the stairs and railing thickness, are supported at each level by a single granite pillar. The wide banister rails are made up of cut slabs of the same material. Contrary to the south staircase, this one retains its very original painted plaster coat imitating a brick bond (paradoxically covering real brick), highlighted with fake cut stone simulating limestone stereotomy♦. One often considers this staircase, incorrectly, as an auxiliary one; it was reserved for the suite of Le Veneur private apartments, whilst the grander ceremonial staircase served the "public" spaces of the dwelling. Since the era of the General who had the kitchen installed in its present location, it was used by the domestics of the château for dining-room duty.

7

Dining-room

With the dining-room (created by the General who installed it around 1787) began the *enfilade* of grand apartments. Until then, no room served a particular dining function, the table being set up according to needs.
A window was enlarged to offer the possibility of gaining direct access to the gardens by a foot bridge fitted above the trench.
The late 16th-century monumental chimneypiece in Maine marble, polished granite and limestone, recalls the Le Veneur family with its mention of the "escutcheon of the comtes [...] Tannegui Le Veneur". A sketch from around 1830 by Godard, Alençon engraver, shows an escutcheon, now missing. The walls are painted with a rag-finish whitewash and marbling.
The tapestry represents the encounter between Abraham and the three strangers. On a large mahogany table is set the General's surtout in gilt bronze, cut crystal and glass.
The Directory chairs have been restored.
Between fountains on painted canvas, the paired portraits of Marie Blosset and Philippe Le Veneur face those of Anne Le Veneur and François de Fiesque, her husband.
The floor is paved in terra-cotta which the General had ordered in Argentan.

Large dish from the General's table service (also comprising four smaller dishes and a large surtout with mirrored back in four sections). Cut crystal and gilt bronze, early 19th century (coll. CMN).

Sketch of the chimneypiece by Godard, circa 1830 (Bibliothèque d'Alençon).

Queen Marie Leszczinska,
pastel by Nattier.

♦ ***Domino:*** *"domino" wall paper is an assembly of rectangular sheets which, when juxtaposed, form a decorative ensemble.*

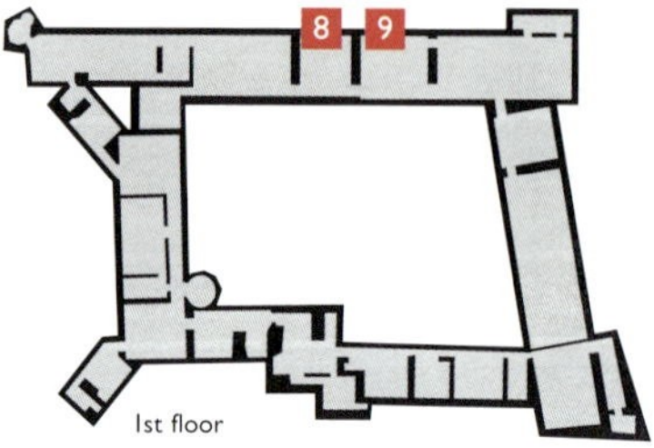

8

Summer salon

This highly intimate room is the smallest one on this floor. Its name derives from the fact that the salon was deprived of a fireplace.
A recent restoration transformed it into a charming little games room enlivened by walls covered in "domino" wall paper♦ with large arabesque motifs in the style of Louis XVI following the Rouen tradition. Furniture of the 18th century – commode, secretaries, hot-water bottle table, desk with tabletop for backgammon with a double-sided board for checkers and chess – complements the fine ensemble of chairs.
The pastel portraits present members of the family living in the 18th century. That of queen Marie Leszczinska, by Nattier, was offered by the queen to president Hénault, uncle of one of the Le Veneur ladies.
The parquet is laid out in a herring-bone pattern called "*point de Hongrie*".

9

Portrait salon

One moves on to the portrait salon where fourteen Le Veneur generations are reunited in a presentation executed in the early 1950s, in continuity with the family tradition. As was the case with most of the other house portraits, on them the General had inscribed the name and titles of each of his ancestors. This "gallery" of couples offers interest more for the diversity and precision of dress than for the quality of the paintings themselves. Most of the personages also figure in the other rooms. For a long time this room served as ceremonial chamber where the General installed himself. The granite chimneypiece with polychrome designs retains its 17th-century vividness. Walls were painted in matching colours imitating cloth. Furniture is disposed around the circumference of the space as was the tradition when it was not in use. The chairs, 19th-century copies, are in Louis-XIII style. The third tapestry of hangings from Sébastien de la Planche's workshop features Jacob interpreting the dream of Pharaoh. On the floor, a chevroned parquet of "*point de Hongrie*" is affixed with wrought-iron nails.

Oil lamp with Le Veneur monogram coiffed by a wrought-iron bouquet. Sketch by Godard, around 1830 (Bibliothèque d'Alençon).

Comte d'Aubeterre de Jonzac, uncle of one of the Le Veneur wives.

10

Grand salon

The room with immense proportions called the 'grand salon' was created during the course of the 19th century by the unification of two salons whose wall partition was removed. Illuminated on three sides, it benefits from full luminosity which accentuates the pale yellow tones of the small-panelled wainscotting.
A granite chimneypiece, slightly austere, was retained whilst another chimney, situated between the two *cabinets* or study doors, disappeared under wall panelling. Behind, in the recess of the south pavilion, three *cabinets* (for resting, reading, writing, confidences ...) were built in. Furniture of the 17th- and 18th-century decorate the space. Gaming tables and chairs are scattered about as though ready to receive guests.

Three Regency commodes and gilt-wood consoles complete the ensemble.
The standing portrait of the cardinal faces king Louis XIV, the latter displayed over the mantel. On the list of precious objects which the General noted at his Paris domicile figures the portrait of comte d'Aubeterre de Jonzac, lieutenant-general of the army, represented in the uniform of brigadier, a rank corresponding to infantry colonel before the Revolution. A "Versailles" parquet is laid down facing the chimneypiece; a combination "Versailles" and "Chantilly" indicates the emplacement of the other salon. Like the other ceremonial rooms, the grand salon was serviced by the ceremonial staircase.

The grand salon, as seen in a 1910 postcard, combines singularly disparate furniture.

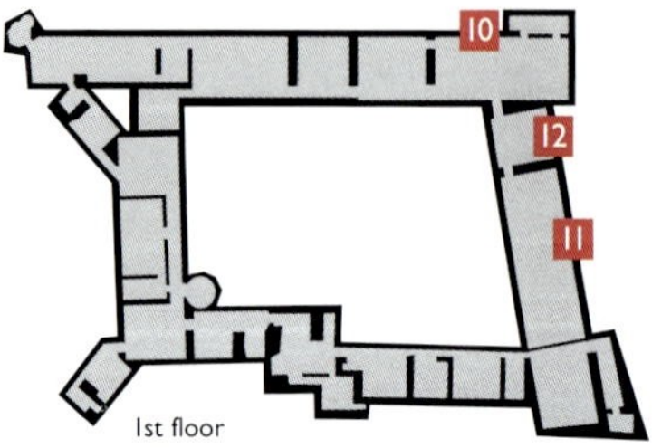

11

Festival hall

Carrouges is one of the rare châteaux to possess a hall for the theatre. This purpose prefigures the current cultural vocation of the monument.
The largest and only two-storey room of the house, 20-metres long by 7-metres wide, the hall occupies the entire gallery wing between the west bastion and south pavilion.
In 1653, this space, on the first floor, was designated as a "paintings gallery". Next to the family portraits appeared works painted by Albani, Guido Reni and Guerchino commissioned in Italy by Jacques Le Veneur. These are no longer in the château.
At the end of the *Ancien Régime*, it was General Le Veneur who undertook the creation of a theatre hall. To give it volume, the upper storey was knocked down, compromising the stability of the construction. As the walls spread apart, beams with reinforced wrought-iron bars were installed, replaced by more discrete tie rods in the 1980s. Mouldings to frame the large panels, window clamps and partition ornaments are the sole elements surviving from the original décor which perhaps included curtains or painted canvas on the wall and a plastered ceiling with moulded frame. During the 1980s restoration, a choice was made to mount chestnut-wood panelling directly on the carpentry members, forming a basket-handled arch.
At the rear opens the salon Pompadour, "foyer" of the theatre; above is located the tribune or platform for musicians.
The wall opposite the ceremonial staircase retains traces of two chimneypieces and the door to the second floor.
The theatre hall was used for comedy and opera. In 1818, the General listed "costumes and effects" reserved for them. Music subscriptions conserved in the archives witness the continuity of family musical practices.
The festival hall has kept its vocation for amusements and reception.

The original ceremonial staircase was entirely plastered, as shown in this postcard from the 1910s.

12

Ceremonial staircase

At the south corner of the château, the landing of the grand staircase assures the junction between the "grand apartments" wing and that of the "gallery". The staircase is a virtuoso composition in brick whose function doubtlessly leant itself more toward ceremony than did its homologue to the east. Despite this more prestigious role, its design is less innovative. The flights turning in the wide, square stair well are separated from the central light by guard rails and ramped arcades supported by four brick piers occupying the total height of the work and playing a unifying role. A granite band runs under the springing of the vaults, whilst rectangular slabs serve as handrail.
The guard-rail shells delimiting the central void are enriched by remarkable decorated panels framed by brick mouldings.

Painted plaster (removed in the 1960s), identical to that still covering the vaults of the east staircase, unified and masked this subtle stereotomy in brick which lends the nickname "Toulousian staircase" to this work.

Gardens

To this day, not one document informs us about the state of the immediate environs of the château before the end of the 16th century. We do not know when major terracing projects occurred to permit the planning of this area. Transformations were likely executed by Tanneguy I to accompany the creation of the new wings around 1575. By the mid-1600s, Jacques Le Veneur commissioned wrought-iron works to compartmentalize the gardens. Some fixed grilles and multiple wrought-iron and fretwork gates are still in situ, exceptional *chefs-d'oeuvre* of the blacksmith's art in the *Grand Siècle*.
The image of a very manicured park with courts, green walls, terraces, parterres, woods, orchards, kitchen gardens, bird breeding, all and more documented by the plan of 1711. Later, the General, encouraged by his mother-in-law, benefactress of Jean-Jacques Rousseau, envisaged a transformation of the park. A plan drafted in 1818 shows a certain number of changes: to the right of the châtelet, transfer of the colonnade of the pond which had just been drained; abandonment of the *broderie*♦ parterres♦; plantation of trees in alignment. As witness to his torrent of activity, Alexis Le Veneur has left us numerous sketches from his hand. One does not know if they remained as proposals or were executed. From the 1950s started renovations to the ten-hectares park, little maintained since the end of the 19th century.
In 1988, a conservatory apple orchard was planted under the care of the natural regional park of Normandy-Maine. Within the bird-breeding garden, flowers are cultivated for bouquets which adorn the salons in season.
In 1999, one of the aviaries, copied from the 1711 plan, was re-established.
A study of the design unity for restoration of the garden was executed in 1989. It relied on the 1711 plan which took into account the condition of the estate at the end of its most brilliant period.
The trees in alignment, chestnuts for the most part, ageing or stricken, were the object of sanitary cropping in 1998 and 1999. Rehabilitation work was initially begun in the year 2000. It is necessary to let time work its way at Carrouges to recuperate the arboured walls and compartmentalized parterres.

♦ ***The little parterre:*** *level space in a garden occupied by flower-beds; detail on the 1711 plan.*

♦ ***Broderie:*** *broad, level areas of a garden with intertwined geometric patterns, usually of boxwood, divided symmetrically by paths.*

Châtelet entry

Seen from the town of Carrouges, the proud silhouette of the little fortified gatehouse attracts attention, contrasting with the more austere lines of the dwelling. Perfectly symmetrical, composed of a central cubic main corps (whose ground-floor is pierced by an entry passage) and confined by four round turrets, it is coifed by a central roof with steep slopes occupying more than half its total height. This pavilion could appear to be of little use if it was not identified as a habitable site by the importance of its windows and the presence of an immense chimney stack.

It is to cardinal Le Veneur that we can attribute this architectural caprice, the sole contribution, it seems, which he left at Carrouges. For the first time, black-brick ornamentation against a red-brick background was applied here, to be extended across the ensemble of new wings erected around fifty years later: lozenges, chevrons, and hearts, blazon, ecclesiastical insignia, and crosses, too.

The window bays carry the richest sculpted decoration at Carrouges.

The châtelet's composition remains Gothic, even though the softened forms approach Renaissance-type volutes and acanthus.

Chapter house

The ancient canons residence of the lords of Carrouges, a little to the north-east of the château, no longer belongs to the estate. Today it houses the headquarters of the natural regional park of Normandy-Maine. Jean Blosset and his wife Marguerite de Derval wished to secure their salvation and give advantage to the prestige of their seigniory by creating a collegiate dedicated to Notre-Dame-de-Bon-Confort. It was to be served by three chaplains and a cleric sharing an annual rent of 65 *livres*, with five more *livres* set aside for illuminations and ornaments. In 1492, six canons were named, the first dignitary of the collegiate being chosen from members of the family. In all seasons, the matins were said at 6 o'clock and the Saturday mass, dedicated to the repose of Louis XI's soul, was celebrated, until the dispersion of the religious under the Revolution. Founded in 1480, the chapter church is a rectangular building which conserves its original carpentry and roof panelling. A lateral chapel, to the south, was used by the lords and became the site of both private sanctuary and funerary chapel. Its rich ornamentation of carved, gilded and painted limestone was executed by Maurice Gabriel and his assistants from October 1642. It was restored after the church itself in the 1980s. Refurbished in the last century, a small funerary enclosure containing the tombs of the Le Veneur family and a few more ancient slab stones adjoin this chapel. The ensemble of lodgings were reserved for the monks. The house facing the sanctuary retains some monumental chimneypieces and exposed beam ceilings, finely moulded. The agricultural buildings (from which the religious community derived its revenue) were renovated in the 19th century. The chapter, deprived of its servants, became a simple farmhouse.

The décor of the Le Veneur private chapel at the collegiate of Carrouges, contemporary to the woodwork ornaments at the château, was executed in painted and gilt limestone, with added marble tablets. Only the lower third of the chapel, set at the height of a man, has a revetment of carved wainscotting.

A short bibliography

Berges (Louis),
Château de Carrouges, Chartrier et papiers de la famille Le Veneur (1394-1925), Conseil général de l'Orne, departmental archives, Alençon, 1995.

Despierres (Mme G.),
Le Château de Carrouges (Orne). Sa chapelle, ses sculptures du XVIIe siècle, Paris, Plon, Nourrit, 1893, 30 pp.
Les Gabriel, recherche sur les origines provinciales de ces architectes, Paris, Plon, 1895.

Lagrange (Jean-Louis) and Taralon (Jean),
"Le château de Carrouges", *Congrès archéologique de France*, 1953, Orne, pp. 317-349.

Rousseau (Xavier),
"Carrouges: la bourgade, les seigneurs, la collégiale, le château", *Le Pays d'Argentan*, 1937, pp. 1-103.
Le Château de Carrouges, Alençon, Imp. Corbière et Jugain, 2nd and 3rd ed., n.d., 67 pp.

Siguret (Philippe),
"Le château de Carrouges", *Monuments historiques*, n° 6.

Since (Marie-Hélène),
"François Gabriel, un architecte novateur à la fin du XVIe siècle en Basse-Normandie", *Bulletin de la Société historique et archéologique de l'Orne*, t. 109, n° 4, 1991, pp. 49-71.
"Les escaliers de Carrouges", *Revue de l'art*, 1993, pp. 62-63.

Captions

CMN (formerly CNMHS): Centre des monuments nationaux.

Cover:
1st: donjon, bridge and entry portal, west bastion.
4th: square paving tile with the Le Veneur monogram.
1st interior overleaf: grille of the ceremonial gate.
2nd interior overleaf: sketch by Godard, circa 1830 (Bibliothèque d'Alençon).

Visit
• Background: detail of a tapestry conserved at the château.

Chronology
Left to right and top to bottom:
• Political life: Horace Vernet, *Bataille de Bouvines*, Versailles, Musée national du Château, Giraudon; "Recueil d'Arras", *Portrait de Louis XI*, Arras, Bibliothèque municipale, Giraudon; François or Jean Clouet, *Portrait de François Ier*, Paris, Musée du Louvre, Lauros-Giraudon; frontispiece of the Haute-Justice de Carrouges with Le Veneur arms, photo C. Terrier; geneology of the Le Veneur family, *Armoiries nouvelles données par Napoléon*, photo C. Terrier.
• Lords: *Portrait posthume de Philippe Le Veneur*, Château de Carrouges, A. Lonchampt/CNMHS; François Clouet, *Portrait de Catherine de Médicis*, Paris, Musée Carnavalet, Lauros-Giraudon; Philippe de Champaigne, *Buste de Louis XIII*, Paris, Musée Carnavalet, Giraudon; *Portrait d'Alexis Le Veneur en 1789*, Château de Carrouges, P. Corbière/Service régional de l'Inventaire général de Basse-Normandie.
• Building: *Émail Plantangenêt*" (detail), Le Mans, Musée de Tessé, grille of the ceremonial gate, sketch by Godard, Bibliothèque d'Alençon, photo C. Terrier; the bridge and entry door, photo C. Terrier.
• Environment: donjon of Chambois, M.H. Since/Conservation régionale des Monuments historiques de Basse-Normandie; vault of the Cathedral of Sées, M.H. Since/Conservation régionale des Monuments historiques de Basse-Normandie; Château de Fervaques, M.H. Since/Conservation régionale des Monuments historiques de Basse-Normandie; clocktower of Saint-Germain d'Argentan, M.H. Since/Conservation régionale des Monuments historiques de Basse-Normandie.

Photographic credits

Alençon, Archives départementales de l'Orne/André Morin: pp. 6t, 10t, 14t, 17b; CNMHS, Archives photographiques: pp. 24, 32t, 35t, 35b, 43b, 45t, 50; CNMHS/Philippe Berthé: pp. 10-11b; CNMHS/Pascal Lemaître: pp. 1t, 46, 47t, 48t, 49b, 52b; CNMHS/Alain Lonchampt: 1st cover, 1st overleaf, geneology (Marie Blosset, General Le Veneur), pp. 1b, 2-3, 7t, 8, 12, 15, 18, 20, 21, 22, 23b, 27t, 28-29, 30, 31, 33, 34, 39, 41, 42, 43t, 44t, 45b, 48b, 51, 52t, 53t, 53b, 54t, 54b, 55t, 55b, 4th cover; CNMHS/Étienne Revault: p. 40t; Giraudon: p. 9; Musées du Mans: p. 6b; Service régional de l'Inventaire général de Basse-Normandie/Pascal Corbière: geneology (all except Marie Blosset and General Le Veneur), pp. 13, 23t, 25l, 43m, 44b, 47bl, 50t, 50m; photos Claude Terrier: 2nd overleaf, pp. 7b, 11t, 14b, 16t, 16b, 17, 25r, 26t, 26m, 26b, 27b, 32b, 36-37, 38, 40b, 47br, 49t.

Editorial coordination and documentation
Chloé Demey

Translator
Barbara Shapiro Comte

Copy editor
Pyra Wise

Design
Atalante/Paris

Graphic design
Atelier des éditions du patrimoine

Graphic information
Didier Hébert
Thierry Renard

Photoengraving
Quattro/Cuincy

Printing
Néo-Typo/Besançon

Dépôt légal: July 2002